THE
Holy Hour
twelve complete services

redemptorist
p u b l i c a t i o n s

The Holy Hour

Published by **Redemptorist Publications**
Alphonsus House, Chawton, Hampshire, GU34 3HQ
Email rp@rpbooks.co.uk, www.rpbooks.co.uk

A registered charity limited by guarantee.
Registered in England 3261721

Copyright © Redemptorist Publications 2018
First published May 2018

Compiled by: Denis McBride C.Ss.R.,
Royston Price C.Ss.R. and Ellen McBride.

Editor: Peter Edwards
Design: Eliana Thompson

ISBN 978-0-85231-514-9

The publisher gratefully acknowledges permission to use the following copyright material:

Excerpts from the English translation and chants of *The Roman Missal* © 2010, International Commission on English in the Liturgy Corporation. All rights reserved.

Excerpts from the *New Revised Standard Version of the Bible: Anglicised Edition*, © 1989. 1995, Division of Christian Education of the National Council of the Churches of Christ in the United States of America. Used by permission. All rights reserved.

Psalms from the Grail Psalter reprinted by permission of HarperCollins Publishers Ltd © 1963.

Taizé songs © Ateliers et Presses de Taizé, 71250 Taizé, France.

Hail Redeemer, King Divine (80905) Text: 77 77 with refrain; Patrick Brennan, 1877–1952, © OCP. All rights reserved. Used with Permission.

Every effort has been made to trace copyright holders and to obtain their permission for the use of copyright material. The publisher apologises for any errors or omissions and would be grateful for notification of any corrections that should be incorporated in future reprints or editions of this book.

Printed and bound by John Dollin Printing Services Ltd, Whitchurch, Hants, RG28 7BB

Contents

Preface

Approaching the presence of the one we love and who loves us is always very special. We may, however, sometimes experience a jumble of emotions: fascination, delight, serenity, a feeling of awkwardness at what to say, nerves on the brink, perhaps nursing a sense of unworthiness or harbouring a measure of past guilt. Who knows what we bring to these moments? We might review in our head how we have managed to get this far, wondering how we have arrived at this signature moment in the relationship. But, for all that, here we are in the presence of the one we love and the one who loves us.

We get to know people best by relating to them. In the pages of the four Gospels there is no full paragraph where Jesus is alone: we do not learn about Jesus in the Gospels by staring at him. The evangelists show us that we learn about Jesus through understanding how he relates to people, what he brings to that relationship, how he comes as blessing or challenge, and how people react differently to him and his values. The evangelists' question is a silent one: who would we be standing beside in the different Gospel scenes?

Because of his deeds and words Jesus evokes a range of responses: jealousy at the success of his ministry; open aggression at his way of eating with sinners; desperation from those longing to be touched by him; suspicion about whom he works for; curiosity about the source of his wisdom; delight at the way he speaks with authority and confronts religious officials; thanksgiving for his healing touch; love and gratitude for his power to change people; fear that his mission is heading for the killing fields; uneasiness when witnessing his vulnerability in Gethsemane; embarrassment and protest at being thought his disciple; sympathy for his suffering on the Via Dolorosa. The list goes on and on. The evangelists turn us away from an exclusive focus on the person of Jesus to attend to how he relates to people and how they relate to him. We learn best about Jesus through those who have life in his name.

Christianity begins in a relationship. We should, of course, experience this for ourselves: we know Jesus best by relating to him.

When we come into the presence of Jesus in the Blessed Sacrament we can bring a litany of different feelings: what hurts us or what haunts us; what delights us and what distresses us; what we secretly hunger for and what we dread most in life. Who knows what people bring in through the doorway of a church or what secret burdens they carry? But picture for a moment coming into the presence of the one who already knows our fears, our awkwardness, our weaknesses, our secret compulsions and the whole story of our life. Imagine coming into the presence of the one who knows us better than we know ourselves and, in spite of all that, stubbornly loves us.

And, dear reader, stop imagining: because this is true in the presence of our beloved Lord.

When we come into the presence of Jesus we come face to face with our redeemer who looks on us with love. We have not come into a courtroom to argue a defence; nor have we entered an arena of accusation. We come home to the Lord and to ourselves, in humility and honesty, without either pretence or affectation. He is the way, the truth and the life: he will show us the way; he will gradually lead us into the truth; he will surely share his life with us. The beauty of being in the presence of the Lord is that it is both comforting and challenging: his assurance of welcome does not disregard the shadow side of our lives. Like the tax-collector Zacchaeus in the Gospel of Luke, the comfort of Jesus' presence allows us to face ourselves more honestly. In the loving regard of the Lord we can see ourselves more clearly.

In 1745 St Alphonsus Liguori wrote the following passage in his *Visits to the Blessed Sacrament*:

> Many Christians make great efforts and put themselves in great danger to visit the sites of the Holy Land, where our most loving Saviour was born, suffered and died. We do not need to make such a long voyage or face so many dangers. The same Lord is near us and lives in the church but a few steps from our homes. Pilgrims consider it a great fortune, says St Paulinus, to bring back a bit of dust from holy sites such as the nativity or the sepulchre where Jesus was buried. Shouldn't we visit the Most Blessed Sacrament where the same Jesus is in person, and where we can safely go with little effort?

This, I think, is beautifully observed. I have been to the Holy Land countless times, leading priests and religious around what one scholar called the Fifth Gospel – the land of Jesus. It was always a memorable time, but wherever we travelled to uncover the footsteps of Jesus, I was always haunted by the angels' annunciation: "He is not here; he is risen." We were not archaeologists hunting for signs of a former presence; we were disciples who believed that the Lord is risen and has given us a perpetual memorial of himself in the Eucharist.

St Alphonsus, the founder of the Redemptorists, is surely right: the Lord is near and waits for us in the Blessed Sacrament. We can visit our loving Lord present to us: in the gathered silence we can speak and we can listen. This is not just remembering a historical presence; this is living presence, here and now. We can celebrate his presence among us not only in the Eucharist when we receive him, but at a Holy Hour service when we visit the real sacramental presence of the Lord unveiled and visible to us in the monstrance. What a privilege to come into the presence of our beloved Lord.

Please permit me to add a note of thanks. In compiling these twelve services I would like to acknowledge the help of my confrère Royston Price C.Ss.R. and my sister Ellen McBride, both of whom have added greatly to the structure and the overall content of these services. Thanks also to Canon Andrew McKenzie of the archdiocese of Glasgow and Canon Edward Pereira of the archdiocese of Southwark for their insightful and helpful comments on how to improve the composition and the choice of the hymns and the texts of the readings. I am deeply grateful to all of them.

Denis McBride C.Ss.R.
Publishing Director
Redemptorist Publications

Holy Hour 1
Peace

EXPOSITION

Entrance hymn and procession

The King of love my shepherd is,
whose goodness faileth never;
I nothing lack if I am his
and he is mine for ever.

Where streams of living water flow
my ransomed soul he leadeth,
and where the verdant pastures grow
with food celestial feedeth.

Perverse and foolish oft I strayed
but yet in love he sought me,
and on his shoulder gently laid,
and home, rejoicing, brought me.

In death's dark vale I fear no ill
with thee, dear Lord, beside me;
thy rod and staff my comfort still,
thy cross before to guide me.

Thou spread'st a table in my sight,
thy unction grace bestoweth:
and O what transport of delight
from thy pure chalice floweth!

And so through all the length of days
thy goodness faileth never;
good shepherd, may I sing thy praise
within thy house for ever.

Henry William Baker (1821–77)

During the last stanza the priest/deacon exposes the
Blessed Sacrament on the altar and returns to kneel
before the Blessed Sacrament.

Opening prayer

Let us pray.
Our Lord Jesus Christ,
we bless you with full hearts
that you are truly present in the Blessed Sacrament on
    this altar.
You welcome everyone who comes to visit you,
whatever our condition, whatever our trials and troubles,
whatever our small triumphs.
We come before you as we are:
you see us better than we see ourselves.
Teach us the joy of living in your presence,
the contentment of gazing upon you,
the delight of knowing that as we look on you,
you have first looked on each of us with love.
Give us peaceful hearts
as we give thanks to you in your holy name,
    Jesus Christ our Lord.

All: **Amen.**

All now sing:

O salutaris hostia
quae caeli pandis ostium:
bella premunt hostilia,
da robur, fer auxilium.

Uni trinoque Domino
sit sempiterna gloria,
qui vitam sine termino
nobis donet in patria.
Amen.

or

14

O saving victim, opening wide
the gate of heaven to us below:
our foes press on from every side;
thine aid supply, thy strength bestow.
To thy great name be endless praise,
immortal Godhead, one in three!

O grant us endless length of days
in our true native land with thee.
Amen.

St Thomas Aquinas wrote the hymn "Verbum Supernum Prodiens" – of which
"O Salutaris Hostia" is the last two stanzas – for the new feast of Corpus
Christi that was extended to the universal Church by Pope Urban IV in 1264.

During the singing, the priest/deacon puts incense on
the charcoal, then incenses the Blessed Sacrament.

ADORATION

After a moment of quiet the priest/deacon or a reader
prays in words from Psalm 121:

I rejoiced when I heard them say:
"Let us go to God's house."
And now our feet are standing
within your gates, O Jerusalem.

Jerusalem is built as a city
strongly compact.
It is there that the tribes go up,
the tribes of the Lord.

For Israel's law it is,
there to praise the Lord's name.
There were set the thrones of judgment
of the house of David.

For the peace of Jerusalem pray:
"Peace be to your homes!
May peace reign in your walls,
in your palaces, peace!"

For love of my brethren and friends
I say: "Peace upon you."
For love of the house of the Lord
I will ask for your good.

The priest/deacon now retires to pray.

Time of quiet for ten minutes.

Reading from Psalm 139

Reader 1:

O Lord, you search me and you know me,
you know my resting and my rising,
you discern my purpose from afar.
You mark when I walk or lie down,
all my ways lie open to you.

Before ever a word is on my tongue
you know it, O Lord, through and through.
Behind and before you besiege me,
your hand ever laid upon me.
Too wonderful for me this knowledge,
too high, beyond my reach.

Sung response by congregation:

O come, let us adore him,
O come, let us adore him,
O come, let us adore him,
Christ the Lord.

Silence for a few minutes.

O where can I go from your spirit,
or where can I flee from your face?
If I climb the heavens, you are there.
If I lie in the grave, you are there.

If I take the wings of the dawn
and dwell at the sea's furthest end,
even there your hand would lead me,
your right hand would hold me fast.

Sung response by congregation:
O come, let us adore him,
O come, let us adore him,
O come, let us adore him,
Christ the Lord.

Silence for a few minutes.
If I say: "Let the darkness hide me
and the light around me be night,"
even darkness is not dark for you
and the night is as clear as the day.

For it was you who created my being,
knit me together in my mother's womb.
I thank you for the wonder of my being,
for the wonders of all your creation.

Sung response by congregation:
O come, let us adore him,
O come, let us adore him,
O come, let us adore him,
Christ the Lord.

Silence for a few minutes.
Already you knew my soul,
my body held no secret from you
when I was being fashioned in secret
and moulded in the depths of the earth.

Your eyes saw all my actions,
they were all of them written in your book;
every one of my days was decreed
before one of them came into being.

Sung response by congregation:
O come, let us adore him,
O come, let us adore him,
O come, let us adore him,
Christ the Lord.

Silence for a few minutes.

To me, how mysterious your thoughts,
the sum of them not to be numbered!
If I count them, they are more than the sand;
to finish, I must be eternal, like you.

O search me, God, and know my heart.
O test me and know my thoughts.
See that I follow not the wrong path
and lead me in the path of life eternal.

Sung response by congregation:

O come, let us adore him,
O come, let us adore him,
O come, let us adore him,
Christ the Lord.

Silence for a few minutes.

Reader 2
(pausing for a few moments between each saying):
We now reflect prayerfully on some of the Gospel
sayings of Jesus.

- Come to me, all you that are weary and are
  carrying heavy burdens, and I will give you rest.
  For my yoke is easy, and my burden is light.

- I am the bread of life. Whoever comes to me
  will never be hungry, and whoever believes in
  me will never be thirsty.

- Anyone who comes to me I will never drive away.

- Love one another as I have loved you.

- Blessed are the meek, for they will inherit
  the earth.

- Blessed are the merciful, for they will receive
  mercy.

- Has no one condemned you?... Neither do I condemn you. Go your way, and from now on do not sin again.

- I am the vine, you are the branches. Those who abide in me and I in them bear much fruit.

- Do not let your hearts be troubled. Believe in God, believe also in me.

- I am the way, and the truth, and the life. No one comes to the Father except through me. If you know me, you will know my Father also.

- I am the living bread that came down from heaven.

- Peace I leave with you; my peace I give to you. I do not give to you as the world gives. Do not let your hearts be troubled, and do not let them be afraid.

Time for quiet reflection.

Reader 3:

A psalm for...
(name a country or city that has suffered a recent tragedy)
To you, Lord, we lift up our eyes,
you who dwell in the midst of us.
We pray for the peace of...,
for the people who suffer and grieve.

Let violence not engulf the people,
crush their villages in darkness and day.
Turn, Lord, and show them your mercy,
redeem them from oppression.

Though anguish and distress have seized them,
though their eyes watch through the night,
though their homes are turned to ruins,
let your face shine upon them.

You who protect the widow and the orphan,
protect the poor and the needy:
do not turn your face away
nor stop your ears to their cries.

Let justice flourish like the cedar of Lebanon,
let peace flow like the rivers from Mount Hermon.
We bless you from this house of the Lord,
that people might know your love has no end.

Brief period of silence.

Towards the end of the Holy Hour the priest/deacon
approaches the altar, genuflects before the Blessed
Sacrament, kneels and invites the assembly to pray.

The Divine Praises

Blessed be God.
Blessed be his Holy Name.
Blessed be Jesus Christ, true God and true Man.
Blessed be the Name of Jesus.
Blessed be his Most Sacred Heart.
Blessed be his Most Precious Blood.
Blessed be Jesus in the Most Holy Sacrament of the Altar.
Blessed be the Holy Spirit, the Paraclete.
Blessed be the great Mother of God, Mary most Holy.
Blessed be her Holy and Immaculate Conception.
Blessed be her Glorious Assumption.
Blessed be the name of Mary, Virgin and Mother.
Blessed be St Joseph, her most chaste spouse.
Blessed be God in his Angels and in his Saints. Amen.

BENEDICTION

The "Tantum Ergo" is now sung.

Therefore we, before him bending,
this great sacrament revere;
types and shadows have their ending,
for the newer rite is here;
faith, our outward sense befriending,
makes the inward vision clear.

Glory let us give, and blessing
to the Father and the Son;
honour, might, and praise addressing,
while eternal ages run;
ever too his love confessing,
who, from both, with both is one.
Amen.

or

Tantum ergo Sacramentum
veneremur cernui:
et antiquum documentum
novo cedat ritui:
praestet fides supplementum
sensuum defectui.

Genitori, genitoque
laus et iubilatio,
salus, honor, virtus quoque
sit et benedictio:
procedenti ab utroque
compar sit laudatio.
Amen.

These are the last two stanzas
of "Pange, Lingua Gloriosi",
written by St Thomas Aquinas
for Corpus Christi.

During the hymn the priest/deacon incenses the
Blessed Sacrament and then rises to proclaim the
traditional responsory:

Panem de caelo praestitisti eis.
Omne delectamentum in se habentem.

Oremus:
Deus, qui nobis sub sacramento mirabili, passionis
tuae memoriam reliquisti: tribue, quaesumus, ita nos
corporis et sanguinis tui sacra mysteria venerari, ut
redemptionis tuae fructum in nobis iugiter sentiamus.
Qui vivis et regnas in saecula saeculorum.

Amen.

or

You have given them bread from heaven.
Having within it all sweetness.

Let us pray:
O God, who in this wonderful sacrament have left us a
memorial of your passion: grant, we beseech you, that
we may so venerate the sacred mysteries of your body
and blood, as always to be conscious of the fruit of your
redemption. You who live and reign for ever and ever.

Amen.

Blessing with the Sacrament

The priest/deacon kneels and assumes the humeral
veil. He rises, genuflects, approaches the altar,
holds up the monstrance and blesses the assembly.
He then genuflects again.

REPOSITION

The priest/deacon reposes the Blessed Sacrament
in the tabernacle and returns to the front of the altar.

Recessional hymn

Holy God, we praise thy name;
Lord of all, we bow before thee!
All on earth thy sceptre claim,
all in heaven above adore thee;
infinite thy vast domain,
everlasting is thy reign.

Hark! The loud celestial hymn
angel choirs above are raising,
cherubim and seraphim,
in unceasing chorus praising;
fill the heavens with sweet accord:
holy, holy, holy, Lord.

Holy Father, holy Son,
Holy Spirit, three we name thee;
while in essence only one,
undivided God we claim thee;
and adoring bend the knee,
while we own the mystery.

Spare thy people, Lord, we pray,
by a thousand snares surrounded:
keep us without sin today,
never let us be confounded.
Lo, I put my trust in thee;
never, Lord, abandon me.

C.A. Walworth (1820–1900)

Holy Hour 2
Service of Anointing

EXPOSITION

Entrance hymn and procession

Dear Lord and Father of mankind,
forgive our foolish ways:
reclothe us in our rightful mind;
in purer lives thy service find,
in deeper reverence praise,
in deeper reverence praise.

In simple trust like theirs who heard,
beside the Syrian sea,
the gracious calling of the Lord,
let us, like them, without a word,
rise up and follow thee,
rise up and follow thee.

Drop thy still dews of quietness,
till all our strivings cease;
take from our souls the strain and stress,
and let our ordered lives confess
the beauty of thy peace,
the beauty of thy peace.

Breathe through the heats of our desire
thy coolness and thy balm;
let sense be dumb, let flesh retire,
speak through the earthquake, wind and fire,
O still small voice of calm,
O still small voice of calm!

John Greenleaf Whittier (1807–92)

During the last stanza the priest exposes the Blessed
Sacrament on the altar and returns to kneel before
the Blessed Sacrament.

Opening prayer

Priest/deacon:

Let us pray.
Our Lord Jesus Christ, we bless you with full hearts
that you are truly present in the Blessed Sacrament on
    this altar.
You welcome everyone who comes to visit you,
whatever our condition, whatever our trials and troubles,
whatever our joys and small triumphs.
We come before you as we are:
you see us better than we see ourselves.
Reach out to us with your loving arms;
transform us with your healing presence.
Teach us the joy of living in your presence,
the contentment of gazing upon you,
the delight of knowing that as we look on you,
you first looked on each of us with love.
We give thanks to you in your holy name, Jesus Christ
    our Lord.

All: **Amen.**

All now sing:

Be still and know that I am God,
be still and know that I am God,
be still and know that I am God.

I am the Lord that healeth thee,
I am the Lord that healeth thee,
I am the Lord that healeth thee.

In thee, O Lord, I put my trust,
in thee, O Lord, I put my trust,
in thee, O Lord, I put my trust.

Author unknown

During the singing the priest puts incense on the charcoal, then incenses the Blessed Sacrament.

ADORATION

After a period of quiet two readers approach the lectern.

Paul's Canticle of Love

Reader 1:

If I speak in the tongues of mortals and angels
but do not have love,
I am nothing
but a noisy gong or a clashing cymbal.

Reader 2:

If I have powers of prophecy,
and understand all mysteries and knowledge.
And if I have faith even to remove mountains
and have not love,
I am nothing.

Reader 1:

If I give away all my possessions;
if I give my body over to be burned,
but have not love,
I gain nothing.

Reader 2:

Love is patient, is kind;
love is not envious or boastful;
is never arrogant or rude;
it does not insist on its own way,
is not irritable or resentful.

Reader 1:
Love does not rejoice in wrongdoing,
but rejoices in the truth.
Love bears all things, believes all things,
hopes all things, endures all things.

Reader 2:
Love never ends.
Prophecies will come to an end;
tongues will cease;
knowledge will come to an end.

Reader 1:
When I was a child,
I spoke like a child, I thought like a child;
when I became an adult,
I put an end to childish ways.

Reader 2:
Now we see in a mirror, dimly;
then we will see face to face.

Reader 1:
Now I know only in part;
then I will know fully,
even as I am fully known.

Reader 2:
Faith, hope, and love abide,
these three;
and the greatest of these is love.

The congregation respond by singing (three times):

O come, let us adore him,
O come, let us adore him,
O come, let us adore him,
Christ the Lord.

Time of quiet.

Reader 3:
A reading from the letter of St James. *James 5:13-15*

Are any among you suffering? They should pray. Are
any cheerful? They should sing songs of praise. Are any
among you sick? They should call for the elders of the
church and have them pray over them, anointing them
with oil in the name of the Lord. The prayer of faith
will save the sick, and the Lord will raise them up; and
anyone who has committed sins will be forgiven.
The word of the Lord.
Thanks be to God.

Time of quiet.

Prayers of pleading

Reader 1:
The response to "Lord, in your mercy" is "Hear our
prayer."
Lord, in your mercy:
Hear our prayer.

We pray for Christian people throughout the world;
for peace in the Church; for the healing of divisions;
that in faith and unity we may be constantly renewed
for the mission and service of the Gospel.
Lord, in your mercy:
Hear our prayer.

We pray for all those who suffer;
for the victims of war and terror;
of persecution and aggression;
of disaster and accident.
Lord, in your mercy:
Hear our prayer.

We pray for those who have no home place
or hearth to lay their head;
for the lonely and those who are always overlooked;
that all may find strength and hope.
Lord, in your mercy:
Hear our prayer.

We pray for all those who are sick in our community,
those in hospital or those living at home;
for those whose spirit is broken;
for those who turn to us for healing and comfort
that, together in the Lord, they may find wholeness
    and peace.
Lord, in your mercy:
Hear our prayer.

We pray for one another and for ourselves,
that we may be instruments of the Lord's peace and joy.
May we know for ourselves, and mediate to others,
the wholeness and healing of the Lord.
Lord, in your mercy:
Hear our prayer.

Priest:

Gracious Lord, in whose presence we are gathered,
listen with kindness to these our prayers as we make
them in your holy name, Jesus Christ our Lord.

Amen.

Time dedicated to the anointing of those who wish

If possible, and if space allows, the row at the front of the seated congregation is kept empty so that the priests can walk along and easily distribute the sacrament to those who wish. The priests first anoint the forehead and then the hands, saying:

Through this holy anointing
may the Lord in his love and mercy
help you with the grace of the Holy Spirit.
Amen.

May the Lord who frees you from sin
save you and raise you up.
Amen.

During the anointing quiet music is played.

After the anointing the priests wash their hands at the credence table.

The presiding priest now approaches the altar, genuflects before the Blessed Sacrament, kneels and invites the assembly to pray.

BENEDICTION

The "Tantum Ergo" is now sung.

Therefore we, before him bending,
this great sacrament revere;
types and shadows have their ending,
for the newer rite is here;
faith, our outward sense befriending,
makes the inward vision clear.

Glory let us give, and blessing
to the Father and the Son;
honour, might, and praise addressing,
while eternal ages run;
ever too his love confessing,
who, from both, with both is one.
Amen.

or

Tantum ergo Sacramentum
veneremur cernui:
et antiquum documentum
novo cedat ritui:
praestet fides supplementum
sensuum defectui.

Genitori, genitoque
laus et iubilatio,
salus, honor, virtus quoque
sit et benedictio:
procedenti ab utroque
compar sit laudatio.
Amen.

During the hymn the priest incenses the Blessed Sacrament and then rises to proclaim the following prayer:

For all that God can do within us,
for all that God can do without us.
Thanks be to God.

For all in whom Christ lived before us.
For all in whom Christ lived beside us.
Thanks be to God.

For all the Spirit wants to bring us,
for where the Spirit wants to lead us.
Thanks be to God.

We have worshipped the Lord
and received his healing and blessing.
For how the Lord has touched us.
Thanks be to God.

Blessing with the Sacrament

The priest kneels and assumes the humeral veil. He rises, genuflects, approaches the altar, holds up the monstrance and blesses the assembly. He then genuflects again.

REPOSITION

The priest reposes the Blessed Sacrament in the tabernacle and returns to the front of the altar.

Recessional hymn

Guide me, O thou great Redeemer,
pilgrim through this barren land;
I am weak, but thou art mighty;
hold me with thy powerful hand:
bread of heaven, bread of heaven,
feed me till I want no more,
feed me till I want no more.

Open now the crystal fountain,
whence the healing stream doth flow;
let the fire and cloudy pillar
lead me all my journey through:
strong deliverer, strong deliverer,
be thou still my strength and shield,
be thou still my strength and shield.

When I tread the verge of Jordan,
bid my anxious fears subside;
death of death, and hell's destruction,
land me safe on Canaan's side:
songs of praises, songs of praises,
I will ever give to thee,
I will ever give to thee.

W. Williams (1717–91)

Holy Hour 3
The Redeemer

EXPOSITION

Entrance hymn and procession

Hail Redeemer, King divine!
Priest and Lamb, the throne is thine;
King, whose reign shall never cease,
Prince of everlasting peace.
Angels, saints and nations sing:
"Praised be Jesus Christ our King;
Lord of life, earth, sky and sea,
King of love on Calvary!"

King most holy, King of truth,
guide the lowly, guide the youth;
Christ thou King of glory bright,
be to us eternal light.
Angels, saints and nations sing:
"Praised be Jesus Christ our King…"

Eucharistic King, what love
draws thee daily from above,
clad in signs of bread and wine :
feed us, lead us, keep us thine!
Angels, saints and nations sing:
"Praised be Jesus Christ our King…"

King, whose name creation thrills,
rule our minds, our hearts, our wills;
till in peace, each nation rings
with thy praises, King of kings.
Angels, saints and nations sing:
"Praised be Jesus Christ our King…"

Patrick Brennan C.Ss.R. (1877–1952)

During the last stanza the priest/deacon exposes the Blessed Sacrament on the altar and returns to kneel before the Blessed Sacrament.

Opening prayer

Priest/deacon:

Let us pray.
My Lord and Redeemer,
you are here with us in this great sacrament of love,
waiting, calling and receiving all who come to visit you.
Set our hearts on fire with love of you,
and help us bring your warmth to a cold world.
You who live and reign with the Father and the Holy Spirit,
one God for ever and ever.
All: **Amen.**

All now sing the Taizé chant "Laudate Omnes Gentes" (or this can be played):

Laudate omnes gentes,
laudate Dominum.
Laudate omnes gentes
Laudate Dominum. (sung three times)

Music: Jacques Berthier (1923–94)

During the singing the priest/deacon puts incense on the charcoal, then incenses the Blessed Sacrament. The priest/deacon now retires to pray.

ADORATION

After a moment of quiet Reader 1 prays the following from Psalm 63:

O God, you are my God, for you I long;
for you my soul is thirsting.
My body pines for you
like a dry, weary land without water.
So I gaze on you in the sanctuary
to see your strength and your glory.

For your love is better than life,
my lips will speak your praise.
So I will bless you all my life,
in your name I will lift up my hands.
My soul shall be filled as with a banquet,
my mouth shall praise you with joy.

Time of quiet.

Reader 2:

A reading from the prophet Isaiah.   *Isaiah 61:1-2. 10-11*

The spirit of the Lord God is upon me,
because the Lord has anointed me;
he has sent me to bring good news to the oppressed,
to bind up the broken-hearted,
to proclaim liberty to the captives,
and release to the prisoners;
to proclaim the year of the Lord's favour,
and the day of vengeance of our God…

I will greatly rejoice in the Lord,
my whole being shall exult in my God;
for he has clothed me with the garments of salvation,
he has covered me with the robe of righteousness,
as a bridegroom decks himself with a garland,
and as a bride adorns herself with her jewels.
For as the earth brings forth its shoots,
and as a garden causes what is sown in it to spring up,
so the Lord God will cause righteousness and praise
to spring up before all the nations.   **39**

Litany

The response is: Be with them, our Redeemer.
Be with them, our Redeemer.

For all who have lost hope in life.
Be with them, our Redeemer.

For all who are overlooked in life.
Be with them, our Redeemer.

For all who struggle with sickness.
Be with them, our Redeemer.

For all who mourn the loss of loved ones.
Be with them, our Redeemer.

For those enclosed in ancient hurt.
Be with them, our Redeemer.

For all who are approaching death.
Be with them, our Redeemer.

For all who are fleeing danger.
Be with them, our Redeemer.

For all who are homeless and hungry.
Be with them, our Redeemer.

We pray now for a few moments, bringing our own intentions to the Redeemer.

Time of quiet.

Reader 4:

A reflection by St Alphonsus Liguori.

O heart of Jesus, in whose love all the sacraments, but especially the Eucharist, find their source, allow me to speak to you now. I know that here on this altar you still love me just as much as when you died on the cross. O divine Jesus, teach all those who don't know you about yourself, bring all those who have died to you. I adore you, I thank you, I love you, together with all those in heaven or earth who love you. O most pure Jesus, purify my heart of everything that distracts from you, and fill it with your holy love. Take entire possession of my heart, so that all my life I may be united to you, and be able to say with St Paul that nothing can "separate us from the love of God in Christ Jesus our Lord".

Time of quiet.

The following hymn may be read or sung.
Take my life, and let it be
consecrated, Lord, to thee;
take my moments and my days,
let them flow in ceaseless praise.

Take my hands, and let them move
at the impulse of thy love.
Take my feet, and let them be
swift and beautiful for thee.

Take my voice, and let me sing
always, only, for my King.
Take my lips, and let them be
filled with messages from thee.

Take my silver and my gold,
not a mite would I withhold.
Take my intellect, and use
every power as thou shalt choose.

Take my will, and make it thine:
it shall be no longer mine.
Take my heart; it is thine own:
it shall be thy royal throne.

Take my love; my Lord, I pour
at thy feet its treasure store.
Take myself, and I will be
ever, only, all for thee.

Frances Ridley Havergal (1836–79)

Time of quiet.

The priest/deacon now approaches the altar, genuflects before the Blessed Sacrament, kneels and invites the assembly to pray.

The Divine Praises

Blessed be God.
Blessed be his Holy Name.
Blessed be Jesus Christ, true God and true Man.
Blessed be the Name of Jesus.
Blessed be his Most Sacred Heart.
Blessed be his Most Precious Blood.
Blessed be Jesus in the Most Holy Sacrament of the Altar.
Blessed be the Holy Spirit, the Paraclete.
Blessed be the great Mother of God, Mary most Holy.
Blessed be her Holy and Immaculate Conception.
Blessed be her Glorious Assumption.
Blessed be the name of Mary, Virgin and Mother.
Blessed be St Joseph, her most chaste spouse.
Blessed be God in his Angels and in his Saints.
Amen.

BENEDICTION

The priest/deacon approaches the altar and kneels to incense the Blessed Sacrament while the following hymn is sung.

Sweet sacrament divine,
hid in thine earthly home;
lo! Round thy lowly shrine,
with suppliant hearts we come;
Jesus, to thee our voice we raise
in songs of love and heartfelt praise
sweet sacrament divine.

Sweet sacrament of peace,
dear home of every heart,
where restless yearnings cease,
and sorrows all depart.
there in thine ear, all trustfully,
we tell our tale of misery,
sweet sacrament of peace.

Sweet sacrament of rest,
ark from the ocean's roar,
within thy shelter blest
soon may we reach the shore;
save us, for still the tempest raves,
save, lest we sink beneath the waves:
sweet sacrament of rest.

Sweet sacrament divine,
earth's light and jubilee,
in thy far depths doth shine
the Godhead's majesty;
sweet light, so shine on us, we pray
that earthly joys may fade away:
sweet sacrament divine.

Francis Stanfield (1835–1914)

Prayer

Lord, we bless you for this time before the Blessed Sacrament. We ask you, in turn, to bless us with your mercy and kindness. May we always feel the saving power of your redemption in our daily life. This we ask in your holy name, Jesus Christ our Lord.
Amen.

Blessing with the Sacrament

The priest/deacon kneels and assumes the humeral veil. He rises, genuflects, approaches the altar, holds up the monstrance and blesses the assembly. He then genuflects again.

REPOSITION

The priest/deacon reposes the Blessed Sacrament in the tabernacle and returns to the front of the altar.

Recessional hymn

O bread of heaven, beneath this veil
thou dost my very God conceal:
my Jesus, dearest treasure, hail!
I love thee and, adoring, kneel;
each loving soul by thee is fed
with thine own self in form of bread.

O food of life, thou who dost give
the pledge of immortality;
I live, no 'tis not I that live;
God gives me life, God lives in me:
he feeds my soul, he guides my ways,
and every grief with joy repays.

O bond of love that dost unite
the servant to his living Lord;
could I dare live and not requite
such love – then death were meet reward:
I cannot live unless to prove
some love for such unmeasured love.

Beloved Lord, in heaven above,
there, Jesus, thou awaitest me;
to gaze on thee with endless love,
yes, thus I hope, thus shall it be:
for how can he deny me heaven,
who here on earth himself hath given?

St Alphonsus Liguori,
translated by E. Vaughan

Holy Hour 4
Thanksgiving

EXPOSITION

Entrance hymn and procession

Now thank we all our God,
with heart and hands and voices,
who wondrous things hath done,
in whom his world rejoices;
who from our mother's arms
hath blessed us on our way
with countless gifts of love,
and still is ours today.

O may this bounteous God
through all our life be near us,
with ever joyful hearts
and blessed peace to cheer us;
and keep us in his grace,
and guide us when perplexed,
and free us from all ills
in this world in the next.

All praise and thanks to God
the Father now be given,
the Son, and him who reigns,
with them in highest heaven
the one eternal God,
whom heaven and earth adore;
for thus it was, is now,
and shall be evermore.

Martin Rinkhart (1586–1649),
translated by Catherine Winkworth (1827–78)

During the last stanza the priest/deacon exposes the
Blessed Sacrament on the altar and returns to kneel.
He puts charcoal on the incense, then incenses the
Blessed Sacrament.

Opening prayer

Priest/deacon:

Let us pray.
My Lord Jesus Christ,
you are here with us in this great sacrament of love,
waiting, calling and receiving all who come to visit you.
Set our hearts on fire with thanksgiving to you,
and help us bring your warmth to a cold world.
You who live and reign with the Father and the Holy Spirit,
one God for ever and ever.

All: **Amen.**

All now sing (three times):

Benedictus qui venit in nomine Domini.
Hosanna in excelsis.

or

Blessed is he who comes in the name of the Lord.
Hosanna in the highest.

ADORATION

After a moment of quiet the priest/deacon invites
the assembly to pray.

O come, let us adore him,
O come, let us adore him,
O come, let us adore him,
Christ the Lord. (sung three times)

The priest/deacon retires to pray.

Time of quiet.

Thoughtful reading from Psalm 102

Reader 1:

The response is: My soul, give thanks to the Lord.
My soul, give thanks to the Lord.

Reader 1:

My soul give thanks to the Lord,
all my being, bless his holy name.
My soul, give thanks to the Lord
and never forget all his blessings.
My soul, give thanks to the Lord.

Reader 2:

It is he who forgives all your guilt,
who heals every one of your ills,
who redeems your life from the grave,
who crowns you with love and compassion,
who fills your life with good things,
renewing your youth like an eagle's.
My soul, give thanks to the Lord.

Reader 1:

The Lord does deeds of justice,
gives judgment for all who are oppressed.
He made known his ways to Moses
and his deeds to Israel's sons.
My soul, give thanks to the Lord.

Reader 2:

The Lord is compassion and love,
slow to anger and rich in mercy.
His wrath will come to an end;
he will not be angry for ever.
He does not treat us according to our sins
nor repay us according to our faults.
My soul, give thanks to the Lord.

Reader 1:

For as the heavens are high above the earth
so strong is his love for those who fear him.
As far as the east is from the west
so far does he remove our sins.
My soul, give thanks to the Lord.

Brief pause for organ or recorded music.

Reader 2:

As a father has compassion on his sons,
the Lord has pity on those who fear him;
for he knows of what we are made,
he remembers that we are dust.
My soul, give thanks to the Lord.

Reader 1:

As for man, his days are like grass;
he flowers like the flower of the field;
the wind blows and he is gone
and his place never sees him again.
My soul, give thanks to the Lord.

Reader 2:

But the love of the Lord is everlasting
upon those who hold him in fear;
his justice reaches out to children's children
when they keep his covenant in truth,
when they keep his will in their mind.
My soul, give thanks to the Lord.

The Lord has set his sway in heaven
and his kingdom is ruling over all.
Give thanks to the Lord, all his angels,
mighty in power, fulfilling his word,
who heed the voice of his word.
My soul, give thanks to the Lord.

Give thanks to the Lord, all his hosts,
his servants who do his will.
Give thanks to the Lord, all his works,
in every place where he rules.
My soul, give thanks to the Lord!
My soul, give thanks to the Lord.

Time of quiet.

Short reflection

Priest/deacon/reader:

An emigrant moving to a new country sometimes
leaves a token of affection for their loved ones, as
something to remember them by. Jesus Christ,
knowing that he would die on the cross, gave us the
Eucharist, not only as a token of his love, but as the
very gift of himself for our nourishment, a way of
staying with us even after he ascended to heaven. We
thank the Lord for this wonderful gift. In the Blessed
Sacrament we have the presence of our king, our
brother, our Lord, our God, our friend: the one who
loves us most. Jesus Christ gives us his totality, how
do we respond?

Time of quiet.

Litany

The response to the litany is: We thank you, O Lord.
We thank you, O Lord.

For the closeness of your presence.
We thank you, O Lord.

For the values of the Gospel.
We thank you, O Lord.

For the gift of yourself in the Eucharist.
We thank you, O Lord.

For your unconditional love.
We thank you, O Lord.

For your everlasting mercy.
We thank you, O Lord.

For the beauty of your creation.
We thank you, O Lord.

For calling us into being.
We thank you, O Lord.

For our families and friends.
We thank you, O Lord.

For our parish community.
We thank you, O Lord.

For our schools and all who work in them.
We thank you, O Lord.

For the energy of our young people.
We thank you, O Lord.

For the wisdom of the old.
We thank you, O Lord.

For all who care for fragile and vulnerable people.
We thank you, O Lord.

For a few moments we make our own prayers of thanksgiving before the Lord.

Time of quiet.

The priest/deacon now approaches the altar, genuflects before the Blessed Sacrament, kneels and invites the assembly to pray.

The Divine Praises

Blessed be God.
Blessed be his Holy Name.
Blessed be Jesus Christ, true God and true Man.
Blessed be the Name of Jesus.
Blessed be his Most Sacred Heart.
Blessed be his Most Precious Blood.
Blessed be Jesus in the Most Holy Sacrament of the Altar.
Blessed be the Holy Spirit, the Paraclete.
Blessed be the great Mother of God, Mary most Holy.
Blessed be her Holy and Immaculate Conception.
Blessed be her Glorious Assumption.
Blessed be the name of Mary, Virgin and Mother.
Blessed be St Joseph, her most chaste spouse.
Blessed be God in his Angels and in his Saints. Amen.

BENEDICTION

The priest/deacon approaches the altar and kneels
to incense the Blessed Sacrament while "Ave Verum
Corpus" is said or sung.

Ave verum corpus, natum
de Maria Virgine,
vere passum, immolatum
in cruce pro homine:
cuius latus perforatum
fluxit aqua et sanguine:
esto nobis praegustatum
in mortis examine.

O Iesu dulcis, O Iesu pie,
O Iesu, fili Mariae,
miserere mei. Amen.

or

Hail true body, born
of the Virgin Mary,
having truly suffered, sacrificed
on the cross for humankind,
from whose pierced side
water and blood flowed:
Be for us a foretaste of the heavenly banquet
in the trial of death!

O sweet Jesus, O holy Jesus,
O Jesus, son of Mary,
have mercy on me. Amen.

During the hymn the priest/deacon incenses
the Blessed Sacrament and then rises to pray
St Augustine's prayer of commitment.

Let us pray in the words of St Augustine.

Now it is you alone that I love,
you alone that I follow,
you alone that I seek.
you alone that I feel ready to serve,
because you alone rule justly.
It is to your authority alone
that I want to submit.
Command me, I pray,
to do whatever you will,
but heal and open my ears
that I may hear your voice.
Heal and open my eyes
that I may see your will.
Tell me where to look
that I may see you,
and I will place my hope
in doing your will.
Amen.

Blessing with the Sacrament

The priest/deacon kneels and assumes the humeral veil. He rises, genuflects, approaches the altar, holds up the monstrance and blesses the assembly. He then genuflects again.

REPOSITION

The priest/deacon reposes the Blessed Sacrament in the tabernacle and returns to the front of the altar.

Recessional hymn

Lead, kindly light, amid th' encircling gloom,
lead thou me on;
the night is dark, and I am far from home;
lead thou me on.
Keep thou my feet; I do not ask to see
the distant scene; one step enough for me.

I was not ever thus, nor prayed that thou
shouldst lead me on;
I loved to choose and see my path; but now
lead thou me on.
I loved the garish day, and, spite of fears,
pride ruled my will; remember not past years.

So long thy power hath blest me, sure it still
will lead me on,
o'er moor and fen, o'er crag and torrent, till
the night is gone,
and with the morn those angel faces smile,
which I have loved long since, and lost awhile.

John Henry Newman (1801–90)

Holy Hour 5
Advent

EXPOSITION

Entrance hymn and procession

O come, O come, Emmanuel,
and ransom captive Israel,
that mourns in lonely exile here
until the Son of God appear:
Rejoice! Rejoice! Emmanuel
shall come to thee, O Israel.

O come, thou Rod of Jesse, free
thine own from Satan's tyranny;
from depths of hell thy people save,
and give them victory o'er the grave:
Rejoice! Rejoice! Emmanuel
shall come to thee, O Israel.

O come, thou dayspring, come and cheer
our spirits by thine advent here;
disperse the gloomy clouds of night,
and death's dark shadows put to flight:
Rejoice! Rejoice! Emmanuel
shall come to thee, O Israel.

O come, O come, thou Lord of might,
who to thy tribes, on Sinai's height,
in ancient times did'st give the law,
in cloud and majesty and awe:
Rejoice! Rejoice! Emmanuel
shall come to thee, O Israel.

From the "Great O Antiphons" (12th–13th century),
translated by J.M. Neale (1816–66)

During the last stanza the priest/deacon exposes the Blessed Sacrament on the altar and returns to kneel before the Blessed Sacrament.

Opening prayer

Priest/deacon:

Let us pray.

Our Lord Jesus Christ, present here in the sacrament on the altar, you are worthy of all praise and worship and blessing. We adore you especially at this time of Advent as we prepare to celebrate your coming into our world as redeemer. Stir up our hearts, we pray, to be watchful and heedful in preparing for the feast of your birth, so that we might be refreshed by your coming and behold your glory. We make our prayer in your holy name, Jesus Christ our Lord.

All: **Amen.**

The priest/deacon puts incense on the charcoal and then incenses the Blessed Sacrament.

ADORATION

After a few moments of silence the priest/deacon rises and faces the people to offer a brief reflection.

Reflection

Dear brothers and sisters:

Advent is a season when we wait in confidence for the birth of our Lord Jesus. It is a season of expectation, of arrivals, of new encounters. We look for the coming of the Lord; we welcome his arrival; we deepen our faith in the one who is Emmanuel, God with us.

The heart of the Advent season is the recognition that we are a people unashamedly centred on God, waiting for God; we gather to celebrate the coming of

God in Jesus and wait for the return of Jesus at the end of time. As we look back and look forward in the liturgy there is a dissent from the pervading culture that everything that is of value is happening now. We express our belief, through a community setting of narration and performance and worship, that we all have a greater power than ourselves to genuflect before, something grander than our own experience to bow down before, something higher than our own insight to acknowledge, something that is beyond us yet is mysteriously part of ourselves.

During Advent we confess our own incompleteness and acknowledge that there is always more to God than what we can know or believe or sense. In that recognition there is a proclamation of hope in the majestic goodness of God: in waiting we declare our hope in God's kind purposes.

This season of Advent gives us time to reflect, to look back and to look forward. In the presence of the living Lord, let us ask his help to look back with kindness and look forward in hope.

Period of silence and personal prayer.

Invocations

Reader 1:

The response to the prayer is: Hear our prayer.
Hear our prayer.

We pray that this period of Advent
will be a blessed and fruitful time.
We pray we may enter the spirit of this season
by waiting hopefully on the Lord.
Lord, in your kindness:
Hear our prayer.

We pray that the Lord in his kindness
will bless all the people who blessed us
with their encouragement and support,
all those who helped us become who we are.
Lord, in your kindness:
Hear our prayer.

We pray that the good Lord enliven us,
in our turn, to reach out to others,
especially those who hunger
for our constant support.
Lord, in your kindness:
Hear our prayer.

May we comfort those who endure times
    of misfortune
and rejoice with them in their success.
Together may we wait in hope
for the coming of the Lord.
Lord, in your kindness:
Hear our prayer.

We pray that we might rejoice at the birth of every child,
each one made in the image of God.
May each child know the welcome
of being embraced into the family of God.
Lord, in your kindness:
Hear our prayer.

Prayer

Priest/deacon:

Let us pray.
May the God and Father of our Lord Jesus Christ
bless us with the gift of faith in his beloved Son,
that we might ever believe and hope in him.
May God be with us in our times of doubt;
may God accompany us in our times of darkness;
may God console us in our times of despair.
In all that we do and say,
may the loving kindness of our God
go out from us as a blessing to others.
Amen.

Period of silence and personal prayer.

Reading

Reader 2:

A reading from the prophet Isaiah.   *Isaiah 9:2-4. 6-7*

The people who walked in darkness
have seen a great light;
those who lived in a land of deep darkness –
on them light has shined.

Sung response:
Rejoice! Rejoice! Emmanuel
shall come to thee, O Israel.

You have multiplied the nation,
you have increased its joy;
they rejoice before you
as with joy at the harvest,
as people exult when dividing plunder.

Sung response:
Rejoice! Rejoice! Emmanuel
shall come to thee, O Israel.

For the yoke of their burden,
and the bar across their shoulders,
the rod of their oppressor,
you have broken as on the day of Midian.

Sung response:
**Rejoice! Rejoice! Emmanuel
shall come to thee, O Israel.**

For a child has been born for us,
a son given to us;
authority rests upon his shoulders;
and he is named
Wonderful Counsellor, Mighty God,
Everlasting Father, Prince of Peace.

Sung response:
**Rejoice! Rejoice! Emmanuel
shall come to thee, O Israel.**

His authority shall grow continually,
and there shall be endless peace
for the throne of David and his kingdom.
He will establish and uphold it
with justice and with righteousness
from this time onward and for evermore.
The zeal of the Lord of hosts will do this.

Sung response:
**Rejoice! Rejoice! Emmanuel
shall come to thee, O Israel.**

Period of silence and private prayer.

Litany of the Blessed Sacrament

Lord, have mercy upon us,
Christ, have mercy upon us.

Christ, hear us,
Christ, graciously hear us.

God the Father,
have mercy upon us.

God the Son,
have mercy upon us.

God the Holy Spirit,
have mercy upon us.

Holy Trinity, One God,
have mercy upon us.

Blessed Jesus, God and Man,
have mercy upon us.

Jesus, whom the heavens cannot contain, yet are really present on our altars,
have mercy upon us.

Jesus, adored by the heavenly hosts, yet accepting our praises,
have mercy upon us.

Jesus, veiling your majesty, that we may draw near to you,
have mercy upon us.

Jesus, Bread of Life, whoever eats you lives for ever,
have mercy upon us.

Jesus, Good Shepherd, laying down your life for your sheep,
have mercy upon us.

Jesus, giving us your own flesh and blood under the forms of bread and wine,
have mercy upon us.

Jesus, becoming one with us in this holy sacrament,
have mercy upon us.

Jesus, yourself both priest and sacrifice,
have mercy upon us.

Have mercy, O Lord,
and pardon our sins.

Have mercy, O Lord,
and renew our souls.

From measuring your power by our weak understanding,
good Lord, deliver us.

From doubts, distractions and irreverence,
good Lord, deliver us.

From unworthy and unfruitful receiving,
good Lord, deliver us.

From coldness, hardness of heart, and ingratitude,
good Lord, deliver us.

By your blessed body, really present in the Holy Communion,
good Lord, deliver us.

By your precious blood, really present in the cup of blessing,
good Lord, deliver us.

We sinners beseech you to hear us, that we may believe all your truths revealed to us,
hear us, Lord.

That we may acknowledge our absolute subjection to your will,
hear us, Lord.

That we may thankfully adore your goodness,
hear us, Lord.

That we may gratefully respond to your gracious invitations,
hear us, Lord.

That we may approach this mystery in perfect charity with all the world,
hear us, Lord.

That receiving your most sacred body and blood, our souls may dissolve in reverence and love,
hear us, Lord.

That returning from this great sacrament, our hearts may continue recollected in you,
hear us, Lord.

That we may be healed of all infirmities, and strengthened against all relapses,
hear us, Lord.

That as we now adore you veiled in mystery, we may hereafter see you face to face,
hear us, Lord.

Lamb of God, who takes away the sins of the world,
spare us, O Lord.

Lamb of God, who takes away the sins of the world,
spare us, O Lord.

Lamb of God, who takes away the sins of the world,
spare us, O Lord.

Priest/deacon:

Let us pray.

O God, who in this wonderful Sacrament
have left us a memorial of your Passion,
grant us, we pray,
so to revere the sacred mysteries of your Body and Blood,
that we may always experience in ourselves the fruits
  of your redemption.
Who live and reign with God the Father,
in the unity of the Holy Spirit,
one God, for ever and ever.
Amen.

BENEDICTION

The priest/deacon approaches the altar and kneels
to incense the Blessed Sacrament while "Ave Verum
Corpus" is said or sung.

Ave verum corpus, natum
de Maria Virgine,
vere passum, immolatum
in cruce pro homine:
cuius latus perforatum
fluxit aqua et sanguine:
esto nobis praegustatum
in mortis examine.

O Iesu dulcis, O Iesu pie,
O Iesu, fili Mariae,
miserere mei. Amen.

or

Hail true body, born
of the Virgin Mary,
having truly suffered, sacrificed
on the cross for humankind,

from whose pierced side
water and blood flowed:
Be for us a foretaste of the heavenly banquet
in the trial of death!

O sweet Jesus, O holy Jesus,
O Jesus, son of Mary,
have mercy on me. Amen.

During the hymn the priest/deacon incenses the
Blessed Sacrament and then rises to proclaim the
prayer:

Let us pray.

O Lord Jesus Christ, who have gifted yourself to us in
this Blessed Sacrament, we bless you for your kindly
presence among us, a presence which sanctifies each
of us. We now plead with you for the kindness of your
blessing. In your blessing may this time bring us ever
closer to you, so that we might always live as in your
presence. This we ask in your holy name, Jesus Christ
our Lord.
Amen.

Blessing with the Sacrament

The priest/deacon kneels and assumes the humeral
veil. He rises, genuflects, approaches the altar,
holds up the monstrance and blesses the assembly.
He then genuflects again.

REPOSITION

The priest/deacon reposes the Blessed Sacrament in
the tabernacle and returns to the front of the altar.

Recessional hymn

Love divine, all loves excelling,
joy of heaven, to earth come down,
fix in us thy humble dwelling,
all thy faithful mercies crown;
Jesu, thou art all compassion,
pure unbounded love thou art,
visit us with thy salvation,
enter every trembling heart.

Breathe, O breathe thy loving Spirit
into every troubled breast,
let us all in thee inherit,
let us find that second rest:
take away our power of sinning,
Alpha and Omega be,
end of faith as its beginning,
set our hearts at liberty.

Come, almighty to deliver,
let us all thy life receive,
suddenly return, and never,
never more thy temples leave.
Thee we would be always blessing,
serve thee as thy hosts above,
pray, and praise thee without ceasing,
glory in thy perfect love.

Finish then thy new creation,
pure and sinless let us be,
let us see thy great salvation,
perfectly restored in thee;
changed from glory into glory,
till in heaven we take our place,
till we cast our crowns before thee,
lost in wonder, love, and praise!

Charles Wesley (1707–88)

71

Holy Hour 6
Lent

Entrance hymn and procession

Godhead here in hiding, whom I do adore,
masked by these bare shadows, shape and nothing more,
see, Lord, at thy service low lies here a heart
lost, all lost in wonder at the God thou art.

Seeing, touching, tasting are in thee deceived:
how says trusty hearing? That shall be believed;
what God's Son has told me, take for truth I do;
truth himself speaks truly, or there's nothing true.

On the cross thy Godhead made no sign to men,
here thy very manhood steals from human ken:
both are my confession, both are my belief;
and I pray the prayer of the dying thief.

O thou our reminder of Christ crucified,
living Bread, the life of us for whom he died,
lend this life to me then; feed and feast my mind,
there be thou the sweetness man was meant to find.

Jesu, whom I look at shrouded here below,
I beseech thee send me what I thirst for so,
some day to gaze on thee face to face in light
and be blest for ever with thy glory's sight. Amen.

Attributed to St Thomas Aquinas,
translated by Gerard Manley Hopkins

During the last stanza the priest/deacon exposes the Blessed Sacrament on the altar and returns to kneel before the Blessed Sacrament. He puts incense on the charcoal, then incenses the Blessed Sacrament.

Opening prayer

Priest/deacon:

Let us pray.

Our Lord Jesus Christ, present here in the sacrament on the altar, you are worthy of all praise and worship and blessing. We come to adore you at this time of Lent, when we prepare ourselves for the sacred Triduum. As we adore you, help us to grow in appreciation of that paschal mystery of your passion, death and resurrection. We make our prayer in your holy name, Jesus Christ our Lord.

All: **Amen.**

ADORATION

Time of quiet.

Reading

Reader 1:

A reading from Paul's letter
to the Philippians.   *Philippians 2:5-11*

Let the same mind be in you that was in Christ Jesus,
who, though he was in the form of God,
did not regard equality with God
as something to be exploited,
but emptied himself,
taking the form of a slave,
being born in human likeness.
And being found in human form,
he humbled himself
and became obedient to the point of death –
even death on a cross.

74

Therefore God also highly exalted him
and gave him the name
that is above every name,
so that at the name of Jesus
every knee should bend,
in heaven and on earth and under the earth,
and every tongue should confess
that Jesus Christ is Lord,
to the glory of God the Father.

All:

**We adore you, O Christ,
and we bless you;
because by your holy cross
you have redeemed the world.**

Time of quiet.

Psalm 50

Reader 2:

Have mercy on me, God, in your kindness.
In your compassion blot out my offence.
O wash me more and more from my guilt
and cleanse me from my sin.

My offences truly I know them;
my sin is always before me.
Against you, you alone, have I sinned;
what is evil in your sight I have done.

Reader 3:

That you may be justified when you give sentence
and be without reproach when you judge,
O see, in guilt I was born,
a sinner was I conceived.

Indeed you love truth in the heart;
then in the secret of my heart teach me wisdom.
O purify me, then I shall be clean;
O wash me, I shall be whiter than snow.

Reader 2:
Make me hear rejoicing and gladness,
that the bones you have crushed may thrill.
From my sins turn away your face
and blot out all my guilt.

A pure heart create for me, O God,
put a steadfast spirit within me.
Do not cast me away from your presence,
nor deprive me of your holy spirit.

Reader 3:
Give me again the joy of your help;
with a spirit of fervour sustain me,
that I may teach transgressors your ways
and sinners may return to you.

O rescue me, God, my helper,
and my tongue shall ring out your goodness.
O Lord, open my lips
and my mouth shall declare your praise.

Reader 2:
For in sacrifice you take no delight,
burnt offering from me you would refuse,
my sacrifice, a contrite spirit,
a humbled, contrite heart you will not spurn.

In your goodness, show favour to Zion:
rebuild the walls of Jerusalem.
Then you will be pleased with lawful sacrifice,
(burnt offerings wholly consumed),
then you will be offered young bulls on your altar.

Time of quiet.

Gospel reading

The Lord be with you.
And with your spirit.

A reading from the holy Gospel according to John.
Glory to you, O Lord.

John 12:20-21. 23-32

Now among those who went up to worship at the festival were some Greeks. They came to Philip, who was from Bethsaida in Galilee, and said to him, "Sir, we wish to see Jesus"... Jesus answered them, "The hour has come for the Son of Man to be glorified. Very truly, I tell you, unless a grain of wheat falls into the earth and dies, it remains just a single grain; but if it dies, it bears much fruit. Those who love their life lose it, and those who hate their life in this world will keep it for eternal life. Whoever serves me must follow me, and where I am, there will my servant be also. Whoever serves me, the Father will honour."

"Now my soul is troubled. And what should I say – 'Father, save me from this hour'? No, it is for this reason that I have come to this hour. Father, glorify your name." Then a voice came from heaven, "I have glorified it, and I will glorify it again." The crowd standing there heard it and said that it was thunder. Others said, "An angel has spoken to him." Jesus answered, "This voice has come for your sake, not for mine. Now is the judgement of this world; now the ruler of this world will be driven out. And I, when I am lifted up from the earth, will draw all people to myself."

The Gospel of the Lord.
Praise to you, Lord Jesus Christ.

The priest/deacon may give a brief reflection, in words such as the following:

We don't know much about these Greeks, probably Gentile converts to Judaism, coming all the way from their homeland to Jerusalem to participate in the Passover celebrations. It's easy to imagine them as slightly timid, keen in their new faith, but worried that their ethnicity would make them stand out. In all their enthusiasm, though, they seek out this Jesus, this figure that everyone is talking about. It's in response to them, these slightly marginal figures, that Jesus marks his startling change of direction. His hour has now come. That Passover was to be the defining moment in the history of the world: our Lord's passion, death and resurrection.

This Gospel passage is very rich, full of things to ponder, especially here before Jesus in the Blessed Sacrament. The passion of Jesus, Christ being raised up on the cross, this tortuous death, is his time of glorification. His death is to be fruitful, bringing forth an abundance of new life.

We've been drawn here by Jesus to adore him, to spend time with him. Like the Greeks, we've decided in our hearts that "we wish to see Jesus", and here we are.

Lord, you've drawn us to yourself for this period of adoration, help us in our journey this Lent; be with us in our preparations to mark your paschal mystery, and throughout our entire lives as your followers, our Lord and our God.

The priest now retires to pray.

Period of silence and personal prayer.

Intercessions

The response to "Lord, in your mercy" is: "Hear our prayer."
Hear our prayer.

We pray that this season of Lent
will be a fruitful time of preparation,
for the celebration of our Lord's passion,
and renewing our relationship with him.
Lord, in your mercy:
Hear our prayer.

We pray for our local church,
for our Bishop N., all our priests and religious,
for our own parish community
and for all our neighbours.
Lord, in your mercy:
Hear our prayer.

We pray for the universal Church,
for N., our Pope,
and for those areas of the world
where the Church is persecuted.
Lord, in your mercy:
Hear our prayer.

We pray for all those who are ill,
for all our friends and family,
for those who are lonely or troubled,
and for those who have given up hope.
Lord, in your mercy:
Hear our prayer.

We pray for all those who have died,
those who mourn the loss of loved ones,
we pray especially for those who have died suddenly
or in tragic circumstances.
Lord, in your mercy:
Hear our prayer.

Priest/deacon:

Let us pray.
Lord, listen to these our prayers and to the deep needs of our own hearts. May we always come before you with deep confidence in your everlasting kindness and mercy. This we ask through your holy name, Jesus Christ our Lord.
Amen.

Period of silence and personal prayer.

Towards the end of the Holy Hour the priest/deacon approaches the altar, genuflects before the Blessed Sacrament, kneels and invites the assembly to pray.

The Divine Praises

Blessed be God.
Blessed be his Holy Name.
Blessed be Jesus Christ, true God and true Man.
Blessed be the Name of Jesus.
Blessed be his Most Sacred Heart.
Blessed be his Most Precious Blood.
Blessed be Jesus in the Most Holy Sacrament of the Altar.
Blessed be the Holy Spirit, the Paraclete.
Blessed be the great Mother of God, Mary most Holy.
Blessed be her Holy and Immaculate Conception.
Blessed be her Glorious Assumption.
Blessed be the name of Mary, Virgin and Mother.
Blessed be St Joseph, her most chaste spouse.
Blessed be God in his Angels and in his Saints. Amen.

BENEDICTION

The priest/deacon puts incense on the charcoal and incenses the Blessed Sacrament while the following hymn is sung.

When I survey the wondrous cross
on which the Prince of glory died,
my richest gain I count but loss,
and pour contempt on all my pride.

Forbid it, Lord, that I should boast,
save in the death of Christ my God!
All the vain things that charm me most,
I sacrifice them to his blood.

See from his head, his hands, his feet,
sorrow and love flow mingled down!
Did e'er such love and sorrow meet,
or thorns compose so rich a crown?

Were the whole realm of nature mine,
that were a present far too small;
love so amazing, so divine,
demands my soul, my life, my all.

Isaac Watts (1674–1748)

The priest/deacon now rises to pray in the words
of St Columba:

Dearest Lord,
be thou a bright flame before us,
be thou a guiding star above us,
be thou a smooth path beneath us,
be thou a kindly shepherd behind us,
today and evermore.
Amen.

And may your blessing
rest upon us
now and evermore.
Amen.

Blessing with the Sacrament

The priest/deacon kneels and assumes the humeral
veil. He rises, genuflects, approaches the altar,
holds up the monstrance and blesses the assembly.
He then genuflects again.

REPOSITION

Recessional hymn

O sacred head surrounded
by crown of piercing thorn!
O bleeding head, so wounded,
reviled and put to scorn!
Death's pallid hue comes o'er thee,
the glow of life decays,
yet angel hosts adore thee,
and tremble as they gaze.

I see thy strength and vigour
all fading in the strife,
and death with cruel rigour,
bereaving thee of life:
O agony and dying!
O love to sinners free!
Jesus, all grace supplying,
O turn thy face on me.

In this, thy bitter passion,
Good Shepherd, think of me,
with thy most sweet compassion,
unworthy though I be:
beneath thy cross abiding,
forever would I rest;
in thy dear love confiding,
and with thy presence blest.

But death too is my ending;
in that dread hour of need,
my friendless cause befriending,
Lord, to my rescue speed:
thyself, O Jesus, trace me,
right passage to the grave,
and from thy cross embrace me,
with arms outstretched to save.

*13th century,
translated by Ronald Knox*

Holy Hour 7
Holy Week

EXPOSITION

Entrance hymn and procession

Abide with me, fast falls the eventide;
the darkness deepens, Lord, with me abide.
When other helpers fail and comforts flee,
help of the helpless, O abide with me.

Swift to its close ebbs out life's little day;
earth's joys grow dim, its glories pass away;
change and decay in all around I see;
O thou who changest not, abide with me.

I fear no foe, with thee at hand to bless;
ills have no weight, and tears no bitterness.
Where is death's sting? Where, grave, thy victory?
I triumph still, if thou abide with me.

Hold thou thy cross before my closing eyes;
shine through the gloom, and point me to the skies;
heaven's morning breaks, and earth's vain shadows flee:
in life, in death, O Lord, abide with me.

H.F. Lyte (1793–1847)

During the last stanza the priest/deacon exposes the
Blessed Sacrament on the altar and returns to kneel
before the Blessed Sacrament. He puts incense on
the charcoal, then incenses the Blessed Sacrament.
He rises to pray.

Opening prayer

Priest/deacon:

Let us pray.
Shepherd of Israel, hear our prayer.
God of Ephraim and Manasseh,
show your glory for us to see,
stir up your power and come to our aid.

Be here among us in this house,
light in the midst of us,
sure comfort and guide:
tend us and preserve us in your life.

From your heaven look down on this vine;
with tender care you have planted it in our land.
Cherish the stock you have planted with your hand.
May every branch flourish in your charge.

Be here among us in this house,
light in the midst of us,
sure comfort and guide:
tend us and preserve us in your life.

We make our prayer in your holy name, Jesus Christ
our Lord.
All: **Amen.**

The priest/deacon now retires to pray.

ADORATION

Time of quiet.

Reading

Reader 1:

A reading from the prophet Isaiah. *Isaiah 52:13 – 53:12*

See, my servant shall prosper,
he shall be exalted and lifted up,
and shall be very high.

86

Just as there were many who were astonished at him
– so marred was his appearance, beyond human
  semblance,
and his form beyond that of mortals –
so he shall startle many nations;
kings shall shut their mouths because of him;
for that which had not been told them they shall see,
and that which they had not heard they shall contemplate.
Who has believed what we have heard?
And to whom has the arm of the Lord been revealed?

For he grew up before him like a young plant,
and like a root out of dry ground;
he had no form or majesty that we should look at him,
nothing in his appearance that we should desire him.
He was despised and rejected by others;
a man of suffering and acquainted with infirmity;
and as one from whom others hide their faces
he was despised, and we held him of no account.

Surely he has borne our infirmities
and carried our diseases;
yet we accounted him stricken,
struck down by God, and afflicted.
But he was wounded for our transgressions,
crushed for our iniquities;
upon him was the punishment that made us whole,
and by his bruises we are healed.

Brief time of silence.

All we like sheep have gone astray;
we have all turned to our own way,
and the Lord has laid on him
the iniquity of us all.

He was oppressed, and he was afflicted,
yet he did not open his mouth;
like a lamb that is led to the slaughter,

and like a sheep that before its shearers is silent,
so he did not open his mouth.
By a perversion of justice he was taken away.
Who could have imagined his future?
For he was cut off from the land of the living,
stricken for the transgression of my people.
They made his grave with the wicked
and his tomb with the rich,
although he had done no violence,
and there was no deceit in his mouth.

Yet it was the will of the Lord to crush him with pain.
When you make his life an offering for sin,
he shall see his offspring, and shall prolong his days;
through him the will of the Lord shall prosper.
Out of his anguish he shall see light;
he shall find satisfaction through his knowledge.
The righteous one, my servant, shall make many
    righteous,
and he shall bear their iniquities.
Therefore I will allot him a portion with the great,
and he shall divide the spoil with the strong;
because he poured out himself to death,
and was numbered with the transgressors;
yet he bore the sin of many,
and made intercession for the transgressors.

The word of the Lord.
Thanks be to God.

Time of quiet.

Taizé chant
Jesus, remember me when you come into your kingdom.
Jesus, remember me when you come into your kingdom.
(repeat)

Music: Jacques Berthier (1923–94)

A modern psalm

You do not send us your word, Lord,
like a torrent of water
raging in tempest and flood,
sweeping all before its force.

You send us your word
like a soft spring breeze,
like a leaf falling gently to the ground,
like a still small voice that whispers your name.

Stripped of all beauty and form
you came among us as a servant,
suffering among us and for us,
dying that we may find life.

You emptied yourself of honour and glory,
you, first-born of all creation.
You came to our domain lonely and defenceless,
and departed like a seed lying dead on the earth.

The grain of wheat can yield no harvest
until it falls and dies on the land.
Your Son had to die in wind and storm
before coming to life in glory.

He became our living bread,
broken that we might be whole,
that we might know new life
and nourish our tired world.

**Glory be to the Father, and to the Son, and
  to the Holy Spirit:
As it was in the beginning, is now, and ever
  shall be,
world without end.
Amen.**

Silent adoration.

Reading

Our reflection is taken from "Death by Bread Alone"
by Dorothee Sölle.

"Man does not live by bread alone." In fact bread alone
kills us. To live by bread alone is to die a slow death
in which all human relationships are strangled. Of
course, such a death by bread alone doesn't mean that
we cease to exist. Our bodies still function. We still go
about the routines of life; we breathe; we produce.

Death by bread alone means being alone and then wanting
to be left alone; being friendless, yet distrusting and
despising others; forgetting others and then being
forgotten; living only for ourselves and then feeling
neglected; neither crying for another nor being cried
for by another.

I have a neighbour, an elderly childless man whose wife
died not long ago. One day he called me over to show
me some damage, scratches that children had made on
his property with their bicycles. "Just look what they
have done," he said. "This house is all I have."

Man dies by bread alone. My neighbour had worked
for what he had. He lived in that house, took care of
it. "This house is all I have," he had said. Suddenly it
dawned on me that this man was dead. He had died
from no longer having any kind of relationship with
another human being.

That is what Jesus means when he speaks of death by
bread alone. Death is what takes place within us when
we look on others not as gift, blessing or stimulus,
but threat, danger, competition. The parable of the
prodigal son is an example of death by bread alone.

He ended up living on starvation wages, for bread alone. That is why his father spoke of him as being dead. The prodigal son had no human ties. There was no one he could speak to. According to Jesus, this kind of existence cannot be called living.

Jesus took side with life against death. When I seek help against death by bread alone, I turn instinctively to Jesus. For Jesus, natural death is not the greatest enemy. He accepted his own death. What he did not accept was the creeping death he saw in the lives of so many people. That is why he preached: "I have come that you may have life, and have it abundantly."

From The Inward Road and the Way Back
(London: DLT, 1975)

Brief period of silence for personal prayer.

Hymn

Sweet sacrament divine,
hid in thine earthly home;
lo! Round thy lowly shrine,
with suppliant hearts we come;
Jesus, to thee our voice we raise
in songs of love and heartfelt praise,
sweet sacrament divine.

Sweet sacrament of peace,
dear home of every heart,
where restless yearnings cease,
and sorrows all depart,
there in thine ear all trustfully
we tell our tale of misery,
sweet sacrament of peace.

Sweet sacrament of rest,
ark from the ocean's roar,
within thy shelter blest
soon may we reach the shore;
save us, for still the tempest raves,
save, lest we sink beneath the waves,
sweet sacrament of rest.

Sweet sacrament divine,
earth's light and jubilee,
in thy far depths doth shine
thy Godhead's majesty;
sweet light, so shine on us, we pray,
that earthly joys may fade away:
sweet sacrament divine.

Francis Stanfield (1835–1914)

Brief period of silence for personal prayer.

Responses

Priest/deacon:
God of justice, rock of our salvation, keep our hearts and minds open to your beloved Son.

Reader 4:
Let us hold fast to his words and express them in deeds, that our faith may be built on a sure foundation and our lives be judged worthy of you.

Priest/deacon:
God, our very breath, our only hope, in every age you take pity on us and bring new life from dead places.

Reader 4:
Visit your people anew, and raise your Church to new life in these uneasy times. May our shepherds lead your people to new pastures, where everyone will feel safe and secure, and grow in the gift of your peace.

Priest/deacon:
God our redeemer, from every land you call a people to yourself. Yours is the work we do, yours is the message we carry.

Reader 4:
Keep your Church single-minded and faithful to your purposes. Let failure not discourage us, nor success beguile our hearts. Keep us constant to the person of Jesus and to the life of the Gospel.

Priest/deacon:
As we pray here, so let us live.
Through Christ our Lord. Amen.

Priest/deacon:
Lord, listen to these our prayers and to the deep needs of our own hearts. May we always come before you with deep confidence in your everlasting kindness and mercy.
Amen.

Silence for personal prayer.

BENEDICTION

The priest/deacon approaches the altar and kneels
to incense the Blessed Sacrament while "Ave Verum
Corpus" is said or sung.

Ave verum corpus, natum
de Maria Virgine,
vere passum, immolatum
in cruce pro homine:
cuius latus perforatum
fluxit aqua et sanguine:
esto nobis praegustatum
in mortis examine.

O Iesu dulcis, O Iesu pie,
O Iesu, fili Mariae,
miserere mei. Amen.

or

Hail true body, born
of the Virgin Mary,
having truly suffered, sacrificed
on the cross for humankind,
from whose pierced side
water and blood flowed:
Be for us a foretaste of the heavenly banquet
in the trial of death!

O sweet Jesus, O holy Jesus,
O Jesus, son of Mary,
have mercy on me. Amen.

During the hymn the priest/deacon incenses
the Blessed Sacrament and then rises to proclaim
the prayer:

Let us pray.
Lord Jesus Christ,
you are the way, the truth, the life.

Do not let us wander from you who are the way;
nor distrust you who are the truth;
nor rest in any other than you
who are the life.

Teach us to do what we do wisely,
to believe your good news firmly,
to love each other tenderly.

And may the blessing you now give us,
rest upon us this day
and abide with us
for evermore.
Amen.

Blessing with the Sacrament

The priest/deacon kneels and assumes the humeral
veil. He rises, genuflects, approaches the altar,
holds up the monstrance and blesses the assembly.
He then genuflects again.

REPOSITION

The priest/deacon reposes the Blessed Sacrament in
the tabernacle and returns to the front of the altar.

Recessional hymn

O sacred head surrounded
by crown of piercing thorn!
O bleeding head, so wounded,
reviled and put to scorn!
Death's pallid hue comes o'er thee,
the glow of life decays,
yet angel hosts adore thee,
and tremble as they gaze.

I see thy strength and vigour
all fading in the strife,
and death with cruel rigour,
bereaving thee of life:
O agony and dying!
O love to sinners free!
Jesus, all grace supplying,
O turn thy face on me.

In this, thy bitter passion,
Good Shepherd, think of me,
with thy most sweet compassion,
unworthy though I be:
beneath thy cross abiding,
forever would I rest;
in thy dear love confiding,
and with thy presence blest.

But death too is my ending;
in that dread hour of need,
my friendless cause befriending,
Lord, to my rescue speed:
thyself, O Jesus, trace me,
right passage to the grave,
and from thy cross embrace me,
with arms outstretched to save.

13th century,
translated by Ronald Knox

Holy Hour 8
A Half-Hour for Children

This service can be led by a priest, a deacon, or a lay person, referred throughout as the leader. If a lay person leads the service, however, there will no formal blessing with the sacrament.

INTRODUCTION

Leader:

We gather in the name of the Father, and of the Son and of the Holy Spirit.

All: **Amen.**

Leader gives an explanation of why we have adoration, for example:

We know that Jesus loves us very much. He loves our parents and all our friends and is always looking after us.

When Jesus was on earth, even though he knew that he would return to his Father, he decided to leave us a great gift. He did not want to leave us alone. When the bread has become the body of Jesus during Mass, we know that he is with us. When Mass is over, so that we can come to church and spend some time talking to him in prayer, he stays as the Holy Communion host in the tabernacle. There are many people who cannot come to Mass, especially those who are sick or old. Special people called extraordinary ministers of the Eucharist take Jesus to them.

At special times, like now, we bring Jesus from the tabernacle for people to pray to him, to adore him, to thank him, to ask him to help us or people in our families whom we are worried about. At these times we can bring the troubles of our world and our communities to Jesus.

In a few moments the Blessed Sacrament will be brought from the tabernacle. We will have some time of praying out loud together, some time of singing and some time of being with him in silence so that we can speak to him in our hearts.

EXPOSITION
Opening song

Praise him!
Praise him in the morning,
Praise him in the noontime.
Praise him!
Praise him!
Praise him when the sun goes down!

Love him!
Love him in the morning,
Love him in the noontime.
Love him!
Love him!
Love him when the sun goes down!

Serve him!
Serve him in the morning,
Serve him in the noontime.
Serve him!
Serve him!
Serve him when the sun goes down!

Author unknown

During the song the leader exposes the Blessed Sacrament on the altar and returns to kneel before the Blessed Sacrament. If a priest or deacon is presiding, and if incense is to be used, he puts incense on the charcoal, then incenses the Blessed Sacrament.

Opening prayer

Leader:

Let us pray.
Jesus, you are here with us today in a very special way: help us all to love you more and more.
Help us during this time with you
to bring our families and friends,
worries and hopes to you in prayer.
You are our Lord for ever and ever.
Amen.

ADORATION

After a moment of quiet the leader invites the assembly to sing:

O come, let us adore him
O come, let us adore him,
O come, let us adore him,
Christ the Lord. (sung three times)

The leader retires to pray.

Time of quiet.

Reading

Reader:
This is a reading from the Gospel of Matthew when Jesus speaks about the importance of children.

Matthew 18:1-4

At that time the disciples came to Jesus and asked, "Who is the greatest in the kingdom of heaven?" He called a child, whom he put among them, and said, "Truly I tell you, unless you change and become like children, you will never enter the kingdom of heaven. Whoever becomes humble like this child is the greatest in the kingdom of heaven."

Brief reflection

The leader may use words such as the following:

People used to bring their children to Jesus for him to pray with them and bless them. Some of his disciples thought that this was wasting his time, when he had so much to do, but Jesus told them that children were very important, and that no one should keep them from him. Children should come to him to be blessed.

Jesus is here with us now in the Blessed Sacrament on the altar. He knows all about you and your life, he loves you and wants to hear all about your day, your life, everything that's going on. You can talk to him in the quiet of your heart, and tell him anything that you're thinking about or struggling with, and he is here to listen and to bless you. Let's have a little quiet time now for a few minutes so that we can talk to Jesus in our heart.

Time of quiet.

Intercessions

The intercessions take the form of the leader introducing a topic, getting the children to think of the intention (for example, their family, world events, or their community) in silence, then singing the Taizé response, "Jesus, remember me".

Leader:

We're now going to bring our prayers to Jesus. He knows all the things that are in our heart, even when we don't say them out loud. We'll go through some areas to pray about, and you can tell Jesus in silence all about it. Then after each one we'll sing together, "Jesus, remember me".

For the Church, for Pope Francis, for our parish, for... (name priests and deacons), for... (name any religious community that has links to the school or parish), for more young people to serve the Church as priests or nuns.

Pause.

**Jesus, remember me when you come into your kingdom.
Jesus, remember me when you come into your kingdom.**

Music: Jacques Berthier (1923–94)

We think about our world, for the leaders who make important decisions, for peace, for all those who are suffering or have had to leave their homes.

Pause.

**Jesus, remember me when you come into your kingdom.
Jesus, remember me when you come into your kingdom.**

We think about our families, our parents, our brothers and sisters, our grandparents, aunts and uncles and cousins. For all our family, those who are alive and those who have gone to heaven. For those we live with, and those who live far away.

Pause.

Jesus, remember me when you come into your kingdom.
Jesus, remember me when you come into your kingdom.

We think about our friends, all those at our school, for those at any clubs or teams we belong to. For all those that we get on well with, and for anyone we don't like. For all the neighbours who live around us.

Pause.

Jesus, remember me when you come into your kingdom.
Jesus, remember me when you come into your kingdom.

We pray for... (other particular local situations or current affairs that may be of concern).

Pause.

Jesus, remember me when you come into your kingdom.
Jesus, remember me when you come into your kingdom.

Time of quiet.

****

If a priest or deacon is the leader, Benediction of the Blessed Sacrament may now follow.

BENEDICTION

The priest/deacon approaches the altar and briefly explains what is about to happen, for example:

Now we come to the part of our time with Jesus when he gives us a special blessing. You know how when our parish priest blesses us, he makes the sign of the cross over us? Well, Jesus is going to give us his blessing. So while that happens we all kneel, and we think of some special thing that we'd like Jesus to bless, perhaps a member of your family, or someone you know who is in need, or any people who are suffering.

If incense is being used, then the priest/deacon puts incense on the charcoal, incenses the Blessed Sacrament and then rises to pray:

Let us pray.
O God, who in this wonderful Sacrament
have left us a memorial of your Passion:
grant us, we pray,
so to revere the sacred mysteries of your Body and Blood
that we may always experience in ourselves
the fruits of your redemption.
Who live and reign with God the Father
in the unity of the Holy Spirit,
one God, for ever and ever.
Amen.

Blessing with the Sacrament

If a priest or deacon is present, he kneels and assumes the humeral veil. He rises, genuflects, approaches the altar, holds up the monstrance and then blesses the assembly.

****

If the leader is a lay person, the service continues without Benediction.

Leader:

We now bow our heads and join our hands.
Dear Jesus,
we ask you kindly for your blessing
not only on us but on all the children of the world,
especially for those who have no home,
no food, no clean water, and no school.
Amen.

****

REPOSITION

The leader reposes the Blessed Sacrament in the tabernacle and returns to the front of the altar, during which the Taizé song "Eat this bread" is sung three times.

Eat this bread, drink this cup, come to him and never be hungry.

Eat this bread, drink this cup, trust in him and you will not thirst.

Music: Jacques Berthier (1923–94)

Holy Hour 9
From the Vatican

This Holy Hour is based on the service which Pope Francis
followed during the hour of Eucharistic Adoration
in the Vatican Basilica on 2 June 2013.

INTENTIONS FOR PRAYER

The Holy Father has asked that this time of Eucharistic Adoration be offered in particular:

1. For the Church dispersed throughout the world, gathered today as a sign of unity in the Most Blessed Sacrament of the Eucharist. The Lord makes her ever more obedient in listening to his word to present her to the world as ever "more glorious, without speck or wrinkle, but holy and faultless" (Ephesians 5:27). By means of its faithful proclamation, may this saving word resound once more as the bearer of mercy and may it stimulate a renewed commitment of love, to provide pain and suffering with full meaning and to re-establish joy and peace.

2. For all of those who, in different parts of the world, live the suffering of new forms of slavery and who are victims of wars, of the trafficking of human beings, of drugs, of "slave" labour, for children and women who suffer any form of violence. May their silent cry for help find the Church alert, so that, with her eyes fixed upon Christ crucified, she may not forget so many of her brothers and sisters left at the mercy of violence. For all those, too, who find themselves in economic insecurity, especially the unemployed, the elderly, immigrants, the homeless, those in prison, and the marginalised; may the prayer of the Church and her active endeavours to be close to them be a source of comfort to them, of support to their hope, of strength and courage in defending the dignity of the person.

EXPOSITION

During the entrance procession the choir/
congregation sings:

Adoro te devote, latens Deitas,
quae sub his figuris vere latitas;
tibi se cor meum totum subiicit,
quia te contemplans, totum deficit.

Visus, tactus, gustus in te fallitur,
sed auditu solo tuto creditur;
credo quidquid dixit Dei Filius,
nil hoc verbo veritatis verius.

In cruce latebat sola Deitas.
At hic latet simul et humanitas:
ambo tamen credens, atgue confitens,
peto quod petivit latro paenitens.

Iesu, quem velatum nunc aspicio,
oro, fiat illud, quod tam sitio,
ut te revelata cernens facie,
visu sim beatus tuae gloriae.
Amen.

or

Godhead here in hiding, whom I do adore,
masked by these bare shadows, shape and nothing more,
see, Lord, at thy service low lies here a heart
lost, all lost in wonder at the God thou art.

Seeing, touching, tasting are in thee deceived:
how says trusty hearing? That shall be believed;
what God's Son has told me, take for truth I do;
truth himself speaks truly, or there's nothing true.

On the cross thy Godhead made no sign to men,
here thy very manhood steals from human ken:
both are my confession, both are my belief;
and I pray the prayer of the dying thief.

Jesu, whom I look at shrouded here below,
I beseech thee send me what I thirst for so,
some day to gaze on thee face to face in light
and be blest for ever with thy glory's sight. Amen.

Attributed to St Thomas Aquinas,
translated by Gerard Manley Hopkins

During the last stanza the priest/deacon exposes the Blessed Sacrament on the altar and returns to kneel before the Blessed Sacrament.

ADORATION

Silence for adoration and for personal prayer.

Reading

Reader: *John 6:35*

Jesus said to the crowd: "I am the bread of life. Whoever comes to me will never be hungry, and whoever believes in me will never be thirsty."

Prayer

O dear Jesus, you who,
hidden under the veil of the Eucharist,
listen in mercy to our humble prayers,
to present them at the throne of the Most High,
accept now in your kindness the yearnings of our hearts.

Enlighten our understanding,
sustain our wills,
strengthen our fidelity,
and enkindle in our hearts a holy enthusiasm,
so that, overcoming our limits and conquering
 every difficulty,
we may be able to render to you a homage
that is less unworthy of your greatness and of your
 majesty, and more in tune with our anxieties and
 with our holy desires.

All: **Amen.**

Pius XII

Invocations

Reader:

The response to the prayers is: Your love is faithful,
Lord Jesus.
Your love is faithful, Lord Jesus.

Give to our Holy Father, wisdom, firmness and
far-sightedness.
Your love is faithful, Lord Jesus.

Give to your Church numerous holy ministers of
the altar.
Your love is faithful, Lord Jesus.

Give to every baptised person hunger and thirst for your body.
Your love is faithful, Lord Jesus.

Give to those who have sinned the desire for conversion and pardon.
Your love is faithful, Lord Jesus.

Give all of us the consoling experience of knowing and feeling that we are loved by you.
Your love is faithful, Lord Jesus.

Prayer

Priest/deacon:

Divine Redeemer,
Daily Bread,
Life of the world,
may your kingdom come.
Lord of lords,
Jesus in the Eucharist,
lovable Shepherd,
preserve us from all dangers.
Jesus, Good Shepherd,
Jesus, Bread of Life,
Jesus our one and only table,
sacrament of love,
save your people.
We find our joy in you, O blessed Jesus.
Amen.

St John XXIII

Silence for prayerful adoration.

Reading

Reader: *John 6:51*

At that time, Jesus said to the crowd, "I am the living
bread that came down from heaven. Whoever eats of
this bread will live for ever; and the bread that I will
give for the life of the world is my flesh."

Prayer

Priest/deacon:

You are the Christ, the Son of the living God,
you are the one who reveals the invisible God,
the first-born of all creatures,
the foundation of all things;
you are the Master of humanity,
you are the Redeemer,
you were born, you died, and you have risen for us;
you are the centre of history and of the world;
you are the one who knows us and who loves us;
you are the companion and friend of our life;
you are the man of sorrow and of hope;
you are he who must come
and who one day will be our judge
and, we hope, you will be our delight.
Amen.

Blessed Paul VI

Invocations

Reader:

The response to the prayer is: We ask you, hear our prayer.
We ask you, hear our prayer.

Break down all division and discord by the power
of your cross.
We ask you, hear our prayer.

Break down all deceit and falsehood by the light
of your word.
We ask you, hear our prayer.

Break down all rancour and sense of revenge by
the meekness of your heart.
We ask you, hear our prayer.

Break down all selfishness and hardness of heart
by the sweetness of your love.
We ask you, hear our prayer.

Break down every form of violence against human life
by your creative power.
We ask you, hear our prayer.

Prayer

Priest/deacon:

Be close to me still, Lord.
Keep your hand on my head,
but let me also hold up my head under your hand.
Take me as I am,
with my defects, with my sins,
but let me become what you wish me to become
and what I too wish me to become.
Amen.

John Paul I

Silence for adoration and for personal prayer.

Reading

John 6:56-57

At that time, Jesus said to the Jews: "Those who eat my flesh and drink my blood abide in me and I in them. Just as the living Father sent me, and I live because of the Father, so whoever eats me lives because of me."

Prayer

Priest/deacon:

Like the two disciples on the road to Emmaus,
we pray you, Lord Jesus: Stay with us!
You who know our hearts,
do not leave us prisoners of the darkness.
Support us when we are tired,
pardon our sins,
direct our steps along the path of goodness.
Give us the taste for a life which is full,
to make us walk on this earth
as pilgrims full of confidence and joy,
gazing always at the goal of the life which has no end.
Amen.

St John Paul II

Invocations

Reader:

The response to the prayer is: We adore you and we bless you, Lord Jesus.
We adore you and we bless you, Lord Jesus.

You are the eternal Son of the Father.
We adore you and we bless you, Lord Jesus.

You are the one sent by the Father for our salvation.
We adore you and we bless you, Lord Jesus.

You are the sole Saviour of the world.
We adore you and we bless you, Lord Jesus.

You are the way, the truth and the life.
We adore you and we bless you, Lord Jesus.

You are the living bread which has come down
from heaven.
We adore you and we bless you, Lord Jesus.

Prayer

Priest/deacon:

Lord Jesus,
who faithfully visit and fill with your presence
the Church and the history of the human race;
who in the wonderful sacrament of your body
    and blood
make us sharers in your divine life and
give us a foretaste of the joy of eternal life,
we adore you and we bless you.
Prostrate before you, source and lover of life,
really present and living in our midst, we beseech you...
in our expectation that we may live always in you,
in the communion of the Blessed Trinity.
Amen.

Benedict XVI

Silence for adoration and for personal prayer.

BENEDICTION

The "Tantum Ergo" is now sung.

Therefore we, before him bending,
this great sacrament revere;
types and shadows have their ending,
for the newer rite is here;
faith, our outward sense befriending,
makes the inward vision clear.

Glory let us give, and blessing
to the Father and the Son;
honour, might, and praise addressing,
while eternal ages run;
ever too his love confessing,
who, from both, with both is one.
Amen.

or

Tantum ergo Sacramentum
veneremur cernui:
et antiquum documentum
novo cedat ritui:
praestet fides supplementum
sensuum defectui.

Genitori, genitoque
laus et iubilatio,
salus, honor, virtus quoque
sit et benedictio:
procedenti ab utroque
compar sit laudatio.
Amen.

During the hymn the priest/deacon incenses the
Blessed Sacrament and then rises to proclaim/sing
the traditional responsory:

Panem de caelo praestitisti eis.
Omne delectamentum in se habentem.

Oremus:
Deus, qui nobis sub sacramento mirabili, passionis
tuae memoriam reliquisti: tribue, quaesumus, ita nos
corporis et sanguinis tui sacra mysteria venerari, ut
redemptionis tuae fructum in nobis iugiter sentiamus.

Qui vivis et regnas in saecula saeculorum.

Amen.

or

You have given them bread from heaven.
Having within it all sweetness.

Let us pray:
O God, who in this wonderful sacrament have left us a
memorial of your passion: grant, we beseech you, that
we may so venerate the sacred mysteries of your body
and blood, as always to be conscious of the fruit of
your redemption.

You who live and reign for ever and ever.

Amen.

Blessing with the Sacrament

The priest/deacon kneels and assumes the humeral
veil. He rises, genuflects, approaches the altar,
holds up the monstrance and blesses the assembly.
He then genuflects again.

REPOSITION

The priest/deacon reposes the Blessed Sacrament in the tabernacle and returns to the front of the altar.

During the reposition a cantor/choir sings the following chant:

Laudate Dominum omnes gentes;
laudate eum, omnes populi,
quoniam confirmata est
super nos misericordia eius,
et veritas Domini manet in aeternum.

Gloria Patri et Filio et Spiritui Sancto,
sicut erat in principio, et nunc, et semper
et in saecula saeculorum.
Amen.

or

Praise the Lord, all nations;
praise him, all people.
For he has bestowed
his mercy upon us,
and the truth of the Lord endures for ever.

Glory to the Father and to the Son and to the Holy Spirit,
as it was in the beginning, is now, and for ever,
and for generations of generations.
Amen.

Alternatively, the congregation sings the Taizé chant three times:

Laudate Dominum,
laudate Dominum,
omnes gentes,
alleluia.

Music: Jacques Berthier (1923–94)

The priest/deacon returns to the front of the altar and invites the congregation to turn to an image of Mary; the service concludes with singing the "Salve Regina" or praying the "Hail Holy Queen".

Salve, Regina, Mater misericordiae;
vita, dulcedo, et spes nostra, salve.
Ad te clamamus, exsules filii Hevae,
ad te suspiramus, gementes et flentes
in hac lacrimarum valle.
Eia, ergo, advocata nostra, illos tuos
misericordes oculos ad nos converte;
et Iesum, benedictum fructum ventris tui,
nobis post hoc exilium ostende.
O clemens, O pia, O dulcis, Virgo Maria.

or

Hail, Holy Queen, Mother of Mercy!
Hail our life,
our sweetness, and our hope!
To you do we cry,
poor banished children of Eve;
to you do we send up our sighs,
mourning and weeping
in this valley of tears.
Turn, then, most gracious advocate,
your eyes of mercy toward us;
and after this, our exile, show unto us
the blessed fruit of thy womb Jesus.
O clement, O loving, O sweet virgin Mary.

The procession bows to the image of Mary and returns to the sacristy.

Holy Hour 10
Love Divine
(led by a lay person)

EXPOSITION

Entrance hymn

We are gathering together unto him,
we are gathering together unto him.
Unto him shall the gathering of the people be.
We are gathering together unto him.

We are offering together unto him,
we are offering together unto him.
Unto him shall the offering of the people be.
We are offering together unto him.

We are singing together unto him,
we are singing together unto him.
Unto him shall the singing of the people be.
We are singing together unto him.

We are praying together unto him,
we are praying together unto him.
Unto him shall the praying of the people be.
We are praying together unto him.

Author unknown

During the last stanza the leader exposes the
Blessed Sacrament on the altar and then kneels
to the side.

ADORATION

After a few minutes of silence the leader goes to the lectern to read the doxology three times and, after a brief pause, the brief reflection.

Doxology

May the heart of Jesus in the Most Blessed Sacrament be praised, adored and loved, with grateful affection, at every moment, in all the tabernacles of the world, even to the end of time. (three times)

Pause.

A brief reflection from St Alphonsus Liguori.

Many Christians make great efforts and put themselves in great danger to visit the sites of the Holy Land, where our most loving Saviour was born, suffered and died. We do not need to make such a long voyage or face so many dangers. The same Lord is near us and lives in the church but a few steps from our homes. Pilgrims consider it a great fortune, says St Paulinus, to bring back a bit of dust from holy sites such as the nativity or the sepulchre where Jesus was buried. Shouldn't we visit the Most Blessed Sacrament where the same Jesus is in person, and where we can safely go with little effort with even ardour?

Silent adoration.

Reading

A reading from the Second Vatican Council's Dogmatic Constitution on the Church.

The laity are gathered together in the people of God and make up the body of Christ under one head... The lay apostolate is a participation in the salvific mission of the Church itself. Through their baptism and confirmation all are commissioned to that apostolate by the Lord himself. Moreover, by the sacraments, especially holy Eucharist, that charity toward God and humankind which is the soul of the apostolate is communicated and nourished. Now the laity are called in a special way to make the Church present and operative in those places and circumstances where only through them can it become the salt of the earth. Thus every lay person, in virtue of the very gifts bestowed upon them, is at the same time a witness and a living instrument of the mission of the Church itself.

Lumen Gentium *33*

Pause for reflection.

Prayer

Give me, good Lord,
a full faith and a fervent charity,
a love of you, good Lord,
incomparable above the love of myself;
and that I love nothing to your displeasure
but everything in an order to you.

Take from me, good Lord,
this lukewarm fashion,
or rather key-cold manner of meditation
and this dullness in praying to you.
And give me warmth, delight and life
in thinking about you.

And give me your grace
to long for your holy sacraments
and specially to rejoice
in the presence of your blessed body,
sweet Saviour Christ,
in the holy sacrament of the altar,
and duly to thank you
for your gracious coming.

St Thomas More

The congregation sings the following response
three times:

O come, let us adore him,
O come, let us adore him,
O come, let us adore him,
Christ the Lord.

Silent adoration.

Reading

The response is: How lovely is your dwelling place,
Lord, God of hosts.
How lovely is your dwelling place, Lord, God of hosts.

My soul is longing and yearning,
is yearning for the courts of the Lord.
My heart and my soul ring out their joy
to God, the living God.
How lovely is your dwelling place, Lord, God of hosts.

The sparrow herself finds a home
and the swallow a nest for her brood;
she lays her young by your altars,
Lord of hosts, my king and my God.
How lovely is your dwelling place, Lord, God of hosts.

They are happy, who dwell in your house,
for ever singing your praise.
They are happy, whose strength is in you,
in whose hearts are the roads to Zion.
How lovely is your dwelling place, Lord, God of hosts.

As they go through the Bitter Valley
they make it a place of springs
(the autumn rain covers it with blessings).
They walk with ever growing strength,
they will see the God of gods in Zion.
How lovely is your dwelling place, Lord, God of hosts.

O Lord God of hosts, hear my prayer,
give ear, O God of Jacob.
Turn your eyes, O God, our shield,
look on the face of your anointed.
How lovely is your dwelling place, Lord, God of hosts.

One day within your courts
is better than a thousand elsewhere.
The threshold of the house of God
I prefer to the dwellings of the wicked.
How lovely is your dwelling place, Lord, God of hosts.

For the Lord God is a rampart, a shield;
he will give us his favour and glory.
The Lord will not refuse any good
to those who walk without blame.
How lovely is your dwelling place, Lord, God of hosts.

Lord, God of hosts,
happy the one who trusts in you!
How lovely is your dwelling place, Lord, God of hosts.

Silent adoration.

Reader 4:

A prayer for a visit to the Blessed Sacrament
by St Alphonsus Liguori.

My Lord Jesus Christ, who for the love which you bear
    to people,
remain night and day in this sacrament full of compassion
    and of love,
waiting, calling and welcoming all who come to visit you;
I believe that you are truly present in the sacrament of
    the altar.

I adore you humbly, and I thank you
for all the graces which you have bestowed upon me;
in particular for having given me yourself in this sacrament,
for having given me your most holy Mother Mary as my
    mediatrix
and for having called me to visit you in this church.

I salute your most loving heart, and this for three purposes:
first, in thanksgiving for this great gift;
secondly, to make amends to you for all the outrages
which you receive in this sacrament from all your enemies;
thirdly, to adore you, by this visit, in all the places on earth
in which you are present in this sacrament
and in which you are least revered and most abandoned.

My Jesus I love you with my whole heart!

I grieve for having so often offended your infinite goodness.
I promise, by your grace, never more to offend you
and, as unworthy as I am, I consecrate myself to you
    completely;
renouncing my entire will, my affections, my desires,
    and all that I possess.
Do with me as you please and whatever you please
    with all that I have.

Finally, dear Saviour, I unite all my affections with
    those of your most loving heart
and I offer them, thus united, to your eternal Father,
beseeching him in your name because of your love,
to accept them and to grant my petitions.

Hymn

Alleluia, sing to Jesus,
his the sceptre, his the throne;
alleluia, his the triumph,
his the victory alone:
hark! the songs of peaceful Sion
thunder like a mighty flood;
Jesus out of every nation
hath redeemed us by his blood.

Alleluia, not as orphans
are we left in sorrow now;
alleluia, he is near us,
faith believes, nor questions how;
though the cloud from sight received him
when the forty days were o'er,
shall our hearts forget his promise,
"I am with you evermore"?

Alleluia, bread of angels,
thou on earth our food, our stay;
alleluia, here the sinful
flee to thee from day to day;
intercessor, friend of sinners,
earth's redeemer, plead for me,
where the songs of all the sinless
sweep across the crystal sea.

W. Chatterton Dix (1837–98)
This hymn is not suitable for use during Lent

Silent adoration.

The Divine Praises

We now pray the Divine Praises.
Blessed be God.
Blessed be his Holy Name.
Blessed be Jesus Christ, true God and true Man.
Blessed be the Name of Jesus.
Blessed be his Most Sacred Heart.
Blessed be his Most Precious Blood.
Blessed be Jesus in the Most Holy Sacrament of the Altar.
Blessed be the Holy Spirit, the Paraclete.
Blessed be the great Mother of God, Mary most Holy.
Blessed be her Holy and Immaculate Conception.
Blessed be her Glorious Assumption.
Blessed be the name of Mary, Virgin and Mother.
Blessed be St Joseph, her most chaste spouse.
Blessed be God in his Angels and in his Saints. Amen.

In a service led by a lay person there is no solemn blessing with the sacrament.

Leader:

We now bow our heads and ask God to bless us and all those we cherish.

Prayer

Grant us, O gracious Lord,
in all our ways, your help;
in all our uncertainties, your counsel;
in all our trials, your protection;
in all our sorrows, your peace.
Amen.

May the Lord bless us and take care of us;
may the Lord be kind and gracious to us;
may the Lord look on us with favour
and abide with us evermore.
Amen.

REPOSITION

The leader now reposes the Blessed Sacrament in
the tabernacle and returns to the front of the altar.

Recessional hymn

Love divine, all loves excelling,
joy of heaven, to earth come down,
fix in us thy humble dwelling,
all thy faithful mercies crown;
Jesu, thou art all compassion,
pure unbounded love thou art,
visit us with thy salvation,
enter every trembling heart.

Breathe, O breathe thy loving Spirit
into every troubled breast,
let us all in thee inherit,
let us find that second rest:
take away our power of sinning,
Alpha and Omega be,
end of faith as its beginning,
set our hearts at liberty.

Come, almighty to deliver,
let us all thy life receive,
suddenly return, and never,
never more thy temples leave.
Thee we would be always blessing,
serve thee as thy hosts above,
pray, and praise thee without ceasing,
glory in thy perfect love.

Finish then thy new creation,
pure and sinless let us be,
let us see thy great salvation,
perfectly restored in thee;
changed from glory into glory,
till in heaven we take our place,
till we cast our crowns before thee,
lost in wonder, love, and praise!

Charles Wesley (1707–88)

Holy Hour 11
The Body of Christ
(led by a lay person)

EXPOSITION

Entrance hymn

The Lord's my shepherd, I'll not want;
he makes me down to lie
in pastures green; he leadeth me
the quiet waters by.

My soul he doth restore again,
and me to walk doth make
within the paths of righteousness,
e'en for his own name's sake.

Yea, though I walk in death's dark vale,
yet will I fear no ill;
for thou art with me, and thy rod
and staff my comfort still.

My table thou hast furnishèd
in presence of my foes;
my head thou dost with oil anoint,
and my cup overflows.

Goodness and mercy all my life
shall surely follow me;
and in God's house for evermore,
my dwelling place shall be.

From the Scottish Psalter, 1650

During the last stanza the leader exposes the Blessed Sacrament
on the altar and returns to kneel before the Blessed Sacrament.

ADORATION

After a few moments of quiet the leader goes to the lectern.

Leader:
During this Holy Hour we will reflect on the body of Jesus during his earthly ministry. [1]

When we reflect on the last hours of Jesus,
we think, among other things,
about what happens to Jesus' body.
It is a body that is taken, led away, handed over;
a body that is abused, tortured, stripped;
a body that is nailed down to lumber,
raised aloft in the Jerusalem killing fields
and exhibited as a spectacle for the curious.
It is a body violently dismissed to death.

But before Jesus is handed over to his enemies,
he hands himself over, with care, to his friends.
He takes the bread and solemnly says:
"Take and eat, this is my body, given for you."

It is a body given, pledged, bequeathed.
Jesus hands over his body –
not his ideas or his insights or his teachings –
as his final gift to his friends.
There is nothing more personal than this:
his own body is his lasting memorial.
What more could he give?

Sometimes we forget a simple truth:
that it was not only his body that Jesus left us as gift,
but it was through that same body
that he gifted people in his life.

The story of our salvation is told
through the body of Jesus.

1 These reflections are taken from Denis McBride, *Journeying with Jesus* (Chawton: Redemptorist Publications, 2009), pp. 116-21.

Pause.

The congregation responds by singing (three times):

**Laudate omnes gentes,
laudate Dominum.
Laudate omnes gentes,
laudate Dominum.**

*Music: Jacques Berthier
(1923–94)*

Time of quiet.

The eyes of Jesus

Reader 1:

Think of the eyes of Jesus,
those eyes, educated by a magnanimous heart,
that looked out on the sweep of life
and appreciated such loveliness and majesty
where others glimpsed little or none.
Think not only of the word of God come among us
but of the eyes of God that graced the commonplace.

Jesus was not skilled at turning a blind eye
to awkward people or troublesome events.
His eyes were quick to notice so many small things –
like the widow at the treasury in the Temple
who gave not out of her abundance
but from her poverty, everything she possessed.
She was left with nothing but Jesus' lavish wonder.

You watch as the rich young man comes to Jesus,
eager to join him, but then turns away with fallen face
from the unforeseen demands of discipleship.

137

And as he disappears back though the crowd
you watch Jesus steadfastly look after him in love.
The love that Jesus feels and offers, strangely,
is not dependent on the response of others.
His love is not a social contract,
but given without measure or calculation.

Finally, you watch the bruised eyes
under a makeshift crown of thorns
look down from the height of the cross
with forgiveness on those zealous for his death.
Then his sight dissolves with life itself.

Pause.

The congregation responds by singing (three times):

Laudate omnes gentes,
laudate Dominum.
Laudate omnes gentes,
laudate Dominum.

Time of quiet.

The ears of Jesus

Think of the ears of Jesus,
the ears that were assaulted by so many screams for help:
"*Kyrie eleison*: O Lord, take pity upon me!"

Think of this man from Nazareth
who did not stop his ears to people's howling and keening;
who never turned away from strident cries
that interrupted his roadside seminars
with so many part-time students.

No, he was not the unmoved mover of the philosophers,
but the one who was readily touched by the desperate
who yearned to reach the heart of God.

Think of the ears that were baffled and hurt
by the hostile cries of his own townspeople,
by the authorities' accusations, their scorn
and unsparing verdicts. The ears that heard
his principal disciple deny him
to a little maidservant who opened doors in the dark.
At that point, we wonder, could Jesus believe his ears?

The ears that, on the cross, could hear no more cries,
only his own inner howl at being abandoned by God.

Pause.

The congregation responds by singing (three times):

**Laudate omnes gentes,
laudate Dominum.
Laudate omnes gentes,
laudate Dominum.**

Time of quiet.

The touch of Jesus

Think of Jesus' touch,
those hands that reached out and made contact
with a litany of people in gestures of comfort
and welcome and healing.
The hands that mixed spittle and clay,
pressing miracle into the eyes of the blind.

The arms that held up a little child as an icon
as he warned his disciples to leave off
being fascinated with themselves and hierarchy,
but learn to welcome the miniature people.
The hands that received people
rather than dismissing them;
the arms that held without crushing;
the hands that offered bread and wine
and awesome indiscriminate welcome.

Think of the arms that carried the weight of the cross
and needed help to endure the journey;
the hands that were now held back from people
because they were pierced and pinioned to the cross.
The hands that could no longer bear the weight of his body,
which slumped forward into the collapse of death.

Pause.

The congregation responds by singing (three times):

Laudate omnes gentes,
laudate Dominum.
Laudate omnes gentes,
laudate Dominum.

Time of quiet.

The nose of Jesus

Think of Jesus' nose:
we don't know if it was big or small, wide or thin;
but we do know Jesus had a nose for the marginal
  people in life,
the legion of the vulnerable and the broken.
This was the man who never looked down his nose
  at anyone;
the one who never walked around with his nose in the air;
the one who could sniff out hypocrisy and corruption,
just as he could unearth hidden worth in the strangest
  people.

We think of the one who breathed in
the fragrance of the lilies of the field,
and blessed God for the exquisite beauty of life.

We think of the one who had a delightful curiosity
about the world around him
and the people who inhabited it:
so he mixed with, and indeed ate with,
the crooked and the cracked,
the good and the bad, the virtuous and sinners,
thus becoming the most indiscriminate host in history.
He ended up having as his last companions in life
two crucified thieves – retaining his reputation to the end.

Pause.

The congregation responds by singing (three times):

Laudate omnes gentes,
laudate Dominum.
Laudate omnes gentes,
laudate Dominum.

Time of quiet.

The feet of Jesus

Think of the feet of Jesus,
feet that carried him to so many towns and villages;
feet weary and bruised from a nomadic way of life,
walking the rough roads of Galilee and Judaea.

"Foxes have holes and the birds of the air have nests,
but the Son of Man has nowhere to lay his head."

These were the feet that trudged on and on,
without home to reach and rest.
But the feet carried a message,
as the prophet Isaiah proclaimed:

"How beautiful on the mountains
are the feet of those who bring good news,
who proclaim peace,
who bring good tidings,
who proclaim salvation,
who say to Zion, 'Your God reigns!'"

On the night before he died
Jesus aproned himself as a servant,
and sank to his knees to wash the feet of his disciples.
Feet would make his finest homily.

If they missed the point of loving humble service,
of tender intimate devotion, of respect,
no Eucharist or ritual or extravagant liturgy
would ever compensate for that loss.

Liturgy, however grand, becomes suddenly irrelevant
when love is absent from the table.
If they missed that, they missed everything.

His own unwashed homeless feet
would eventually stagger and stumble
under the weight of a cross,
feet that would be spiked to an upright stake,
feet that, all too soon, could no longer buttress him
in life but simply give way in death.

Pause.

The congregation responds by singing (three times):

**Laudate omnes gentes,
laudate Dominum.
Laudate omnes gentes,
laudate Dominum.**

Time of quiet.

The voice of Jesus

Think of Jesus' voice,
a voice that spoke so many words
of tenderness and forgiveness to desolate people,
a voice that challenged and confronted
unyielding religious authorities.
This was not any voice but *vox Dei*, the voice of God,
whose message was so often lost on the wind.

His was the voice that protested against
the Pharisees and the scribes and the chief priests,
challenging them to abandon their practice of inventing
new-fangled burdens for people to carry.
They had become, he said, specialists
at smothering the wavering flame
and crushing the broken reed.

His was a voice that was forever mindful
of those whom life had subdued and defeated:
"Come to me all you who labour
and are overburdened
and I will give you rest."

The mouth that hymned the Beatitudes,
that begged, insisted we love one another
as he surely loves us,
is now given vinegar to drink.
The voice was silenced on Golgotha.

But not for ever.

Pause.

The congregation responds by singing (three times):

Laudate omnes gentes,
laudate Dominum.
Laudate omnes gentes,
laudate Dominum.

Time of quiet.

Jesus' body

This was his body,
and through his body
came the grace of our Lord Jesus Christ.

As Teresa of Avila prayed:
"Christ has no body but yours,
no hands, no feet on earth but yours,
yours are the eyes with which he looks
compassion on this world,
yours are the feet with which he walks to do good,
yours are the hands, with which he blesses all the world.
Yours are the hands, yours are the feet,
yours are the eyes, you are his body.
Christ has no body now but yours,
no hands, no feet on earth but yours,
yours are the eyes with which he looks
compassion on this world.
Christ has no body now on earth but yours."

In that understanding by St Teresa
it is through our bodies that
Jesus ministers to a broken world:
through our eyes; through our touch;
through our ears; through our voice.

We pray, in the words of St Augustine,
that when we gather for the Eucharist
we might become what we eat –
the body of Christ.

Pause.

The congregation responds by singing (three times):

Laudate omnes gentes,
laudate Dominum.
Laudate omnes gentes,
laudate Dominum.

Time of quiet.

In a service led by a lay person there is no solemn blessing with the sacrament.

Leader:

We now bow our heads and ask God to bless us and all those we cherish.

Prayer

Leader:

Soul of Christ, sanctify me.
Body of Christ, save me.
Blood of Christ, inebriate me.
Water from the side of Christ, wash me.
Passion of Christ, strengthen me.
O Good Jesus, hear me.
Within your wounds hide me.
Permit me not to be separated from you.
From the wicked foe, defend me.
At the hour of my death, call me
and bid me come to you
that with your saints I may praise you
for ever and ever. Amen.

Attributed to St Ignatius Loyola

REPOSITION

The leader now reposes the Blessed Sacrament in the tabernacle and returns to the front of the altar.

Recessional hymn

O bread of heaven, beneath this veil
thou dost my very God conceal:
my Jesus, dearest treasure, hail!
I love thee and, adoring, kneel;
each loving soul by thee is fed
with thine own self in form of bread.

O food of life, thou who dost give
the pledge of immortality;
I live, no 'tis not I that live;
God gives me life, God lives in me:
he feeds my soul, he guides my ways,
and every grief with joy repays.

O bond of love that dost unite
the servant to his living Lord;
could I dare live and not requite
such love – then death were meet reward:
I cannot live unless to prove
some love for such unmeasured love.

Beloved Lord, in heaven above,
there, Jesus, thou awaitest me;
to gaze on thee with endless love,
yes, thus I hope, thus shall it be:
for how can he deny me heaven,
who here on earth himself hath given?

St Alphonsus Liguori,
translated by E. Vaughan

Holy Hour 12
The Rosary
(led by a lay person)

EXPOSITION

Entrance hymn

Lord Jesus, think on me,
and purge away my sin;
from earthborn passions set me free,
and make me pure within.

Lord Jesus, think on me,
with care and woe oppressed;
let me thy loving servant be,
and taste thy promised rest.

Lord Jesus, think on me
amid the battle's strife;
in all my pain and misery
be thou my health and life.

Lord Jesus, think on me,
nor let me go astray;
through darkness and perplexity
point thou the heavenly way.

Lord Jesus, think on me,
when flows the tempest high:
when on doth rush the enemy,
O Saviour, be thou nigh.

Lord Jesus, think on me,
that, when the flood is past,
I may the eternal brightness see,
and share thy joy at last.

Synesius of Cyrene (c. 375–430),
translated by A.W. Chatfield

During the hymn the leader exposes the Blessed
Sacrament on the altar and returns to kneel before
the Blessed Sacrament.

ADORATION

After a few moments of quiet the leader goes
to the lectern.

Leader:

During this Holy Hour we will pray and reflect on the
five Sorrowful Mysteries of the Rosary, each focused
on the passion journey of Jesus. Praying the Rosary
means that what is remembered is not lost history
but an abiding force that continues to give meaning to
what is happening now in our lives. The story of Jesus
and Mary is part of our own lives: our story, in turn, is
significant to them.

Reader 1:

THE FIRST MYSTERY:
THE AGONY IN THE GARDEN

Mark 14:32-36

They went to a place called Gethsemane; and Jesus
said to his disciples, "Sit here while I pray." He took
with him Peter and James and John, and began to be
distressed and agitated. And he said to them, "I am
deeply grieved, even to death; remain here, and keep
awake." And going a little farther, he threw himself
on the ground and prayed that, if it were possible, the
hour might pass from him. He said, "Abba, Father, for
you all things are possible; remove this cup from me;
yet, not what I want, but what you want."

The leader prays the first decade with the congregation.

Prayer[1]

Reader 1:

Redeemer of the world,
in spite of your fear and dread
in the garden of Gethsemane
you submitted to do your Father's will
and endure the brutal way of the cross.

Look with merciful kindness on us
when we are weak and wayward;
when our fear decides the roads we take;
when our distress conquers our courage;
when our desolation keeps us from daring.

Grace us with strength and boldness
that we might face our Gethsemane
and find words for our sorrow and pain,
rather than covering our confusion in sleep.

Help us to accept, like you,
that fear and dread
are part of our human makeup
and need not be denied or covered up.
In the midst of all our fear, dear Lord,
may we struggle to do the Father's will.

Time of quiet.

1 The prayers are taken from Denis McBride, *Praying the Rosary: a journey through scripture and art* (Chawton: Redemptorist Publications, 2014), pp. 80, 86, 93, 98, 104.

THE SECOND MYSTERY:
THE SCOURGING AT THE PILLAR

Mark 15:6-15

Now at the festival Pilate used to release a prisoner for them, anyone for whom they asked. Now a man called Barabbas was in prison with the rebels who had committed murder during the insurrection. So the crowd came and began to ask Pilate to do for them according to his custom. Then he answered them, "Do you want me to release for you the King of the Jews?" For he realised that it was out of jealousy that the chief priests had handed Jesus over. But the chief priests stirred up the crowd to have him release Barabbas for them instead. Pilate spoke to them again, "Then what do you wish me to do with the man you call the King of the Jews?" They shouted back, "Crucify him!" Pilate asked them, "Why, what evil has he done?" But they shouted all the more, "Crucify him!" So Pilate, wishing to satisfy the crowd, released Barabbas for them; and after flogging Jesus, he handed him over to be crucified.

The leader prays the second decade with the congregation.

Prayer

Reader 2:

We bless you, dear Lord,
for enduring the violence
of your scourging at the pillar
and the heartless abuse
meted out by your torturers.

When we are in the dark of suffering,
shed your gracious light upon us.
When we are struck by misfortune,
console us with your loving presence.
When our flesh is weak and overburdened,
strengthen our resolve to persevere.
When we feel utterly alone,
assure us of your loving attendance.

We pray for all innocent people
who are tortured in secret
throughout our broken world.
Be with them in their fear and loneliness,
in the agony of their diminishment
and in the face of execution and death.
Forgive all injustice in our lives,
and transform us to act
as instruments of your peace.

It is by your wounds that we are healed.

Time of quiet.

Reader 3:

THE THIRD MYSTERY:
THE CROWNING WITH THORNS

John 19:1-7

Then Pilate took Jesus and had him flogged. And the soldiers wove a crown of thorns and put it on his head, and they dressed him in a purple robe. They kept coming up to him and saying, "Hail, King of the Jews!" and striking him on the face. Pilate went out again and said to them, "Look, I am bringing him out to you to let you know that I find no case against him." So Jesus came out, wearing the crown of thorns and the purple robe. Pilate said to them, "Here is the man!" When the chief priests and the police saw him, they shouted, "Crucify him! Crucify him!" Pilate said to them, "Take him yourselves and crucify him; I find no case against him." The Jews answered him, "We have a law, and according to that law he ought to die because he has claimed to be the Son of God."

The leader prays the third decade with the congregation.

Prayer

Reader 3:

Lord Jesus Christ, holy and merciful one,
you suffered in silence
when you were made the object
of the soldiers' brutal attention;
you were dressed up as a king
with a crown of thorns pressed on your head;
you were tormented and derided,
then paraded as a spectacle
for the entertainment of the mob.

You did not meet violence with violence
but endured what was done to you.
Help us always to reverence
your way, your truth and your forbearance.

Keep us always mindful of your boundless love.

Take from us all bitterness and resentment
towards our fellow human beings;
make us agents of your compassion
to the suffering, the persecuted
and all who are oppressed by violence.
Grace us always with your strength and solace.

Time of quiet.

THE FOURTH MYSTERY:
THE CARRYING OF THE CROSS

Luke 23:26-32

As they led him away, they seized a man, Simon of Cyrene, who was coming from the country, and they laid the cross on him, and made him carry it behind Jesus. A great number of the people followed him, and among them were women who were beating their breasts and wailing for him. But Jesus turned to them and said, "Daughters of Jerusalem, do not weep for me, but weep for yourselves and for your children. For the days will surely come when they will say, 'Blessed are the barren, and the wombs that never bore, and the breasts that never nursed.' Then they will begin to say to the mountains, 'Fall on us'; and to the hills, 'Cover us.' For if they do this when the wood is green, what will happen when it is dry?"

Two others also, who were criminals, were led away to be put to death with him.

The leader prays the fourth decade with the congregation.

Prayer

O holy and loving Redeemer,
by whose wounds we are healed,
by whose cross we are liberated:
when we are called to bear your cross
like Simon of Cyrene of old,
let us rejoice in this privilege
and endure it for your sake.

Be for us our companion on the way,
a support in our weariness,
a shielding in danger,
a shelter in the storm,
a shade in the heat,
an assurance in disappointment.

The Via Dolorosa winds its way
through all the towns and villages in our land,
through every home, past every door.

Help us, dear Lord, to attend with mercy
those who walk their way of the cross:
those who are struck down by misfortune;
those who are afflicted by violence;
those who are abused and oppressed.

Be their light and their guide
this day and always.

Time of quiet.

157

Reader 5:

THE FIFTH MYSTERY:
THE CRUCIFIXION

John 19:25-30

Standing near the cross of Jesus were his mother, and his mother's sister, Mary the wife of Clopas, and Mary Magdalene. When Jesus saw his mother and the disciple whom he loved standing beside her, he said to his mother, "Woman here is your son." Then he said to the disciple, "Here is your mother." And from that hour the disciple took her into his own home.

After this, when Jesus knew that all was now finished, he said (in order to fulfil the scripture), "I am thirsty." A jar full of sour wine was standing there. So they put a sponge full of the wine on a branch of hyssop and held it to his mouth. When Jesus had received the wine, he said, "It is finished." The he bowed his head and gave up his spirit.

The leader prays the fifth decade with the congregation.

Prayer

Beloved Lord Jesus Christ,
who endured the shame and bitterness
of the way of the cross and the crucifixion,
yet reached out beyond your suffering
to unite your family and followers:
kindle in our hearts gratitude
for the love that moves beyond its own pain,
for the kindness that attends the distress of others,
for the forgiveness that releases from bondage.

Grant that we may never presume on your mercy,
but live as people who have been forgiven much.

Help us never to nurse anger or hoard hurt;
make us tender and compassionate towards others
that you might forgive us
as we forgive those who sin against us.

Preserve, dear Lord, in love all those
to whom we are bound by ties of family and affection;
refresh our homes with your abiding presence
and sanctify all our human relationships.
We pray that in the hour of our own trial,
when we are covered in darkness,
we may be strengthened by your kindly light.

Time of quiet.

159

Litany

The response to the litany is: Stay with us, Lord.
All: **Stay with us, Lord.**

When the road is long:
Stay with us, Lord.

When burdens weigh us down:
Stay with us, Lord.

When relationships are hard:
Stay with us, Lord.

When disaster occurs:
Stay with us, Lord.

When forgiveness challenges:
Stay with us, Lord.

When hatred grows:
Stay with us, Lord.

When jealousy destroys:
Stay with us, Lord.

When darkness comes:
Stay with us, Lord.

When nobody cares:
Stay with us, Lord.

When friends abandon us:
Stay with us, Lord.

When hope is a foreign country:
Stay with us, Lord.

When we give up praying:
Stay with us, Lord.

When faith seems onerous:
Stay with us, Lord.

When death approaches:
Stay with us, Lord.

Leader:

We now bow our heads and ask God to bless us and all those we cherish.

In a service led by a lay person there is no solemn blessing with the sacrament.

REPOSITION

The leader now reposes the Blessed Sacrament in the tabernacle and returns to the front of the altar while the final hymn is sung.

Recessional hymn

O sacred head surrounded
by crown of piercing thorn!
O bleeding head, so wounded,
reviled and put to scorn!
Death's pallid hue comes o'er thee,
the glow of life decays,
yet angel hosts adore thee,
and tremble as they gaze.

I see thy strength and vigour
all fading in the strife,
and death with cruel rigour,
bereaving thee of life:
O agony and dying!
O love to sinners free!
Jesus, all grace supplying,
O turn thy face on me.

In this, thy bitter passion,
Good Shepherd, think of me,
with thy most sweet compassion,
unworthy though I be:
beneath thy cross abiding,
forever would I rest;
in thy dear love confiding,
and with thy presence blest.

But death too is my ending;
in that dread hour of need,
my friendless cause befriending,
Lord, to my rescue speed:
thyself, O Jesus, trace me,
right passage to the grave,
and from thy cross embrace me,
with arms outstretched to save.

13th century,
translated by Ronald Knox